A YEAR-LONG BIB

# *Praying*
# THE
# NAMES
# OF GOD

## FOR 52 WEEKS

## EXPANDED EDITION

# ANN SPANGLER

HarperChristian
Resources

*Praying the Names of God for 52 Weeks, Expanded Edition*

© 2023 by Ann Spangler

Published in Grand Rapids, Michigan, by HarperChristian Resources. HarperChristian Resources is a registered trademark of HarperCollins Christian Publishing, Inc.

Requests for information should be addressed to customercare@harpercollins.com.

ISBN 978-0-310-14515-8 (softcover)
ISBN 978-0-310-14516-5 (ebook)

HarperChristian Resources titles may be purchased in bulk for church, business, fundraising, or ministry use. For information, please e-mail ResourceSpecialist@ChurchSource.com.

First Printing February 2023 / Printed in the United States of America

23 24 25 26 27 LBC 11 10 9 8 7

# CONTENTS

CV 11.20.2023 0130

# INTRODUCTION

The Bible reveals many fascinating names and titles for God that can yield rich insights for Bible study. *Praying the Names of God for 52 Weeks* rests on the premise that we can experience God in fresh ways by encountering his names and titles in the Scriptures and by learning about the biblical and cultural context in which these were revealed. But these names and titles, particularly in the Old Testament, may be difficult for lay readers to identify simply by paging through their English translation of the Bible.

*Praying the Names of God for 52 Weeks* allows readers to explore the richness of these names for themselves. Each of the names and titles is presented in English (along with its rendering in Hebrew, Greek, or Aramaic). And each section includes a key Scripture passage revealing the name, helpful background information, and Bible study questions designed for individuals and groups. Each week also include passages and prompts designed to help readers learn how to pray them and to see where the name can be found in Scripture.

Though I have focused on 52 "names of God," I should point out that most of these are more properly called titles. In fact, the name for God in the Old Testament is *Yahweh*, and of course the name for his Son in the New Testament is "Jesus," whose Hebrew name, *Yeshua*, means "*Yahweh* is salvation."

When studying the names of God, it helps to realize that names in the ancient world in which the Bible was written often functioned differently than they do today, at least in the western world. In addition to distinguishing one person from another and linking people to their family heritage, names were thought to reveal the essential nature and character of a person. This is particularly true when it comes to the various names and titles of God revealed in Scripture. Furthermore, it was thought that to know God's name was to enjoy a kind of privileged access to him. Once his people knew his name, they could cry out to him, claiming his help and protection. But God's self-revelation also introduced a note of vulnerability. By associating his name so closely with a particular people, God risked the possibility that they would dishonor it by behaving in ways that contradicted his character.

Names like *Abba*, "Father," *Yahweh Yireh*, "The Lord Will Provide," and *El Shadday*, "God Almighty," spread comfort, hope, and awe, while names like *Esh Oklah*, "Consuming Fire," and *El Kanna*, "Jealous God" challenge us to a purer, more passionate commitment. The same is true for the names and titles of Jesus, which yield a rich and deeper understanding of his character and purpose. Titles like "Bright Morning Star" and "Prince of Peace" are not only beautiful but deeply meaningful, revealing facets of his life and ministry we may have previously overlooked.

This study is drawn from two longer books entitled *Praying the Names of God* and *Praying the Names of Jesus* that I wrote several years ago. Each book contains 26 names or titles, each of which is explored through a brief Bible study and daily devotional readings pertaining to the name. Because some readers may prefer a standalone Bible study rather than a larger work with daily devotions, I combined the Bible studies from both of these "mother books" to create the original version of this study, published in 2009. Now, this new edition has the added benefit of including Bible passages drawn directly from the *Names of God Bible*, which places the Hebrew names of God directly into the English text. This makes it much easier for readers to locate the Hebrew names in their own preferred translation of the Bible. Though the *Names of God Bible* is no longer available in print form, readers may want to consult the online edition at Biblegateway.com, where it can be searched by passage or keywords.

Careful readers may wonder why I do not refer to the Greek titles in the last half of the study as often as I refer to the Hebrew titles in the first half. Many, if not most, of the Scripture passages cited for the Hebrew titles, are found in the Old Testament, which was written in Hebrew. The Scripture passages that are cited to help readers understand and pray with New Testament titles, originally written in Greek, come from both the Old and New Testaments. It seemed confusing to put the Greek title in headers that often contain passages originally written in Hebrew rather than Greek. While not a perfect rationale, I believe handling it this way adds clarity and avoids unnecessary complexity for most readers.

My hope is that all who undertake this study of the names and titles of God will be richly rewarded, recognizing many surprising connections between the Old and New Testaments, revealing a God whose forgiveness, love, and determination to help and to save is utterly consistent. My prayer is that everyone who encounters God's name within the Bible will be led into a deeper experience of his goodness, majesty, and love.

Special thanks for this edition go to Sara Riemersma, Acquisitions Editor for Trade Curriculum at HarperChristianResources. I'm grateful for Sara's enthusiasm and vision for this revised edition. Thanks also to Meredith Hinds for suggesting passages and prayer prompts that did not appear in the original edition. I'm also grateful to Beth Murphy and her team for their marketing expertise and their efforts to help this study find a wide audience. My gratitude extends to my executive assistant, Natalie Hart, who patiently entered my corrections to the final manuscript.

It would be remiss of me were I not to thank Andrea Doering, editorial director of Revell Books, and Brian Vos, executive editor at the Baker Publishing Group for their help and support in publishing *The Names of God Bible*, for which I served as general editor.

Whatever its flaws might be, I hope this year-long Bible study will lead readers into an encounter with God that will increase their longing to know him better.

# GOD, MIGHTY CREATOR

## אֱלֹהִים
### *ELOHIM*

***Elohim*** is the Hebrew word for God that appears in the very first sentence of the Bible. When we pray to ***Elohim***, we remember that he is the one who began it all, creating the heavens and the earth and separating light from darkness, water from dry land, night from day. This ancient name for God contains the idea of God's creative power as well as his authority and sovereignty. Jesus used a form of the name in his agonized prayer from the cross. "About the ninth hour Jesus cried out in a loud voice, '*Eloi, Eloi, lama sabachthani?*'—which means, 'My God, my God, why have you forsaken me?'" (Psalm 22:1 NIV).

## KEY SCRIPTURE

In the beginning **Elohim** created heaven and earth.

—Genesis 1:1

# GOD REVEALS HIS NAME IN SCRIPTURE
## GENESIS 1:1–10, 31

*Open your personal Bible translation and read the same passage. Make note to yourself or use a simple mark in your Bible every time* **ELOHIM** *is the name God uses for Himself.*

In the beginning **Elohim** created heaven and earth.

[2] The earth was formless and empty, and darkness covered the deep water. The **Ruach Elohim** was hovering over the water.

[3] Then **Elohim** said, "Let there be light!" So there was light. [4] **Elohim** saw the light was good. So **Elohim** separated the light from the darkness. [5] **Elohim** named the light *day*, and the darkness he named *night*. There was evening, then morning—the first day.

[6] Then **Elohim** said, "Let there be a horizon in the middle of the water in order to separate the water." [7] So **Elohim** made the horizon and separated the water above and below the horizon. And so it was. [8] **Elohim** named what was above the horizon *sky*. There was evening, then morning—a second day.

[9] Then **Elohim** said, "Let the water under the sky come together in one area, and let the dry land appear." And so it was. [10] **Elohim** named the dry land *earth*. The water which came together he named *sea*. **Elohim** saw that it was good. [31] And **Elohim** saw everything that he had made and that it was very good. There was evening, then morning—the sixth day.

## UNDERSTANDING THE NAME

**ELOHIM** (e-lo-HEEM) is the plural form of *El* or *Eloah*, one of the oldest designations for divinity in the world. The Hebrews borrowed the term El from the Canaanites. It can refer either to the true God or to pagan gods. Though El is used more than 200 times in the Hebrew Bible, Elohim is used more than 2,500 times. Its plural form is used not to indicate a belief in many gods but to emphasize the majesty of the one true God. He is the God of gods, the highest of all. Christians may also recognize in this plural form a hint of the Trinity— Father, Son, and Holy Spirit. **ELOHIM** occurs thirty-two times in the first chapter of Genesis. After that the name Yahweh appears as well and is often paired with **ELOHIM** and, in the NIV, the two together are translated "the Lord God."

## CONNECTING TO THE NAME

1. "Genesis" is a word that can mean "birth," "history of origin," or "gene-alogy." What can you observe about who God is from this passage about beginnings?

2. What can you observe about the world *Elohim* has made?

3. God gave human beings dominion over the earth. How might we honor the Creator in our stewardship of the earth?

4. In what ways do you enjoy and benefit from creation every day?

5. Since God made us in his image, he has instilled in us creative power. What are your creative gifts?

6. *Elohim* seems delighted by what he has made, proclaiming it good and even very good. How does God's assessment of creation shape your own attitude toward the world? Toward yourself?

7. What do you think it means to be created in "the image of God"? How would your life change if you lived with the constant awareness that he created you to bear his image?

## PRAYING A PASSAGE WITH GOD'S NAME

Set all your desire on knowing God as David did in this psalm. Spend a few moments reflecting on God, your mighty Creator. Then pray through Psalm 63:1–4 focusing your mind and heart on **ELOHIM**.

> "O **Elohim**, you are my **Elohim**.
> At dawn I search for you.
> My soul thirsts for you.
> My body longs for you
> In a dry, parched land where there is no water.
> So I look for you in the holy place
> To see your power and your glory.
> My lips will praise you
> because your mercy is better than life itself.
> So I will thank you as long as I live.
> I will lift up my hands to pray in your name."

## PRAYING THE NAME **ELOHIM** FOR MYSELF

Look up and read: Genesis 9:12–17

Rewrite this passage of Scripture into a personal prayer responding to God's promise as Creator God, as *Elohim*, as he dealt with human brokenness and sin.

_____

_____

_____

_____

# PROMISES FROM **ELOHIM**

"Remember, I am with you and will watch over you wherever you go. I will also bring you back to this land because I will not leave you until I do what I've promised you."

—Genesis 28:15

## FOR DEEPER STUDY

*Read the following passages, considering the name* **ELOHIM** *and how its meaning relates to the context of the passage.*

Psalms 18:28; 22:1–5

Isaiah 41:10

# THE GOD WHO SEES ME

## אֵל רֳאִי *EL ROI*

An Egyptian slave, Hagar, encountered God in the desert and addressed him as **El Roi**, "the God who sees me." Notably, this is the only occurrence of El Roi in the Bible.

Hagar's God is the one who numbers the hairs on our heads and who knows our circumstances, past, present, and future. When you pray to **El Roi**, you are praying to the one who knows everything about you.

## KEY SCRIPTURE

Hagar named **Yahweh**, who had been speaking to her, "You Are **El Roi**." She said, "This is the place where I watched the one who watches over me." [14] This is why the well is named Beer Lahai Roi [Well of the Living One Who Watches Over Me]. It is still there between Kadesh and Bered.

—Genesis 16:13–14

# GOD REVEALS HIS NAME IN SCRIPTURE
## GENESIS 16

*Open your personal Bible translation and read the same passage. Make note to yourself or using a simple mark in your Bible whenever* **EL ROI** *is used as God's name.*

[7] The Messenger of **Yahweh** found her by a spring in the desert, the spring on the way to Shur. [8] He said, "Hagar, Sarai's slave, where have you come from, and where are you going?"

She answered, "I'm running away from my owner Sarai." [9] The Messenger of **Yahweh** said to her, "Go back to your owner, and place yourself under her authority." [10] The Messenger of **Yahweh** also said to her, "I will give you many descendants. No one will be able to count them because there will be so many."

[13] Hagar named **Yahweh**, who had been speaking to her, "You Are **El Roi**." She said, "This is the place where I watched the one who watches over me."

## UNDERSTANDING THE NAME

In the ancient world it was not uncommon for an infertile wife to arrange for a slave girl to sleep with her husband so that the family could have an heir. In fact, Ishmael, the son born to Abraham and Hagar, would have been considered Sarah's legal offspring. Hagar and Ishmael might have fared better had Hagar not forgotten her place the moment she learned of her pregnancy. Still, Sarah's treatment of her seems inexcusable and harsh.

In the midst of her difficulties, Hagar learned that **El Roi** (EL raw-EE) was watching over her and that he had a plan to bless her and her son. One of Abraham's grandsons, Esau, married Ishmael's daughter, and it was the Ishmaelite traders (also referred to as Midianite merchants in Genesis 37:26–28), themselves descended from an Egyptian slave, who transported his great-grandson Joseph into slavery in Egypt.

*For an explanation of the name Yahweh, consult week 6.

# CONNECTING TO THE NAME

1. Why do you think the angel of the Lord began his communication with Hagar by questioning her?

2. Describe what Hagar must have been feeling when she fled from Sarah into the desert. What circumstances in your own life have produced similar emotions?

3. What gave Hagar the courage to go back to Sarah and face her again? How might Hagar's demeanor have changed after her encounter with the angel of the Lord?

4. What images come immediately to mind when you hear the name *El Roi*, "The God who sees me" or the "one who watches over me?"

5. Sarah tried to "force God's hand" in order to have a family. Describe a time when you thought God did not see your need and you were tempted to take matters into your own hands? What happened?

6. How have you seen God's mercy emerge from your own misguided attempts to be in charge?

7. How have you experienced *El Roi's* watchful care?

# PRAYING A PASSAGE WITH GOD'S NAME

*Hagar used the name* **EL ROI** *for God in Genesis 16. Those events occurred when her son Ishmael was a baby. In this second passage, which takes place years later, God calls himself Elohim. Still, he sees Hagar and Ishmael in their distress.*

Focus on the name El Roi and what it reveals about God's character as you read Genesis 21:17–19:

¹⁷ **Elohim** heard the boy crying, and the Messenger of **Elohim** called to Hagar from heaven. "What's the matter, Hagar?" he asked her. "Don't be afraid! **Elohim** has heard the boy crying from the bushes. ¹⁸ Come on, help the boy up! Take him by the hand, because I'm going to make him into a great nation."

¹⁹ **Elohim** opened her eyes. Then she saw a well. She filled the container with water and gave the boy a drink.

## PRAYING THE NAME EL ROI FOR MYSELF

Look up and read: Genesis 9:12–16

El Roi is the God who sees you. As you read this passage, realize that nothing can possibly escape His notice. Write a response to God about a particular difficulty in your life. Address him as though he knows exactly what's going on.

_____

_____

_____

_____

_____

## PROMISES FROM **EL ROI**, THE GOD WHO SEES YOU

He will not let you fall.
Your guardian will not fall asleep.
[5] ***Yahweh*** is your guardian.
***Yahweh*** is the shade over your right hand.
[6] The sun will not beat down on you during the day,
nor will the moon at night.
[7] ***Yahweh*** guards you from every evil.
He guards your life.
[8] ***Yahweh*** guards you as you come and go,
now and forever.

—Psalm 121:3, 5-8

## FOR DEEPER STUDY

*Read the following passages, considering the name* **EL ROI** *and how its meaning relates to the context of the passage.*

Genesis 21:1–21

2 Chronicles 16:9

Psalms 33:13–22

Proverbs 15:3

Matthew 6:3–4

WEEK 3

# GOD ALMIGHTY

## אֵל שַׁדַּי
### *EL SHADDAY*

God revealed himself as *El Shadday*, God Almighty, to Abram and told him of the everlasting covenant he was establishing with him and with his descendants. Until the time of Moses, when another divine name was revealed, the patriarchs considered *El Shadday* as the covenant name of God. When we pray to *El Shadday*, we invoke the name of the one for whom nothing is impossible.

### KEY SCRIPTURE

When Abram was 99 years old, *Yahweh* appeared to him. He said to Abram, "I am *El Shadday*. Live in my presence with integrity. [2]I will give you my promise, and I will give you very many descendants.".

—Genesis 17:1-2

# GOD REVEALS HIS NAME IN SCRIPTURE
## GENESIS 17:1–8, 15–18

*Open your personal Bible translation and read the same passage. Make note to yourself or using a simple mark in your Bible where God uses* **EL SHADDAY** *as the name for Himself.*

When Abram was 99 years old, **Yahweh** appeared to him. He said to Abram, "I am **El Shadday**. Live in my presence with integrity. ² I will give you my promise, and I will give you very many descendants." ³ Immediately, Abram bowed with his face touching the ground, and again **Elohim** spoke to him, ⁴ "My promise is still with you. You will become the father of many nations. ⁵ So your name will no longer be Abram [Exalted Father], but Abraham [Father of Many] because I have made you a father of many nations. ⁶ I will give you many descendants. Many nations and kings will come from you. ⁷ I will make my promise to you and your descendants for generations to come as an everlasting promise. I will be your **Elohim** and the God of your descendants. ⁸ I am also giving this land where you are living—all of Canaan—to you and your descendants as your permanent possession. And I will be your **Elohim**."

## UNDERSTANDING THE NAME

The Hebrew **El Shadday** (EL shad-DAI), often translated "God Almighty," may literally be translated "God, the Mountain One." Since many of the gods of the ancient Near East were associated with mountains, early translators may have made an educated guess regarding its meaning. Like the mountains themselves, God is seen as strong and unchanging. **El Shadday** reveals God not only as the one who creates and maintains the universe but who initiates and maintains a covenant with his people. Shadday occurs thirty-one times in the book of Job and seventeen times in the rest of the Bible. In the New Testament, the Greek term Pantokrator is often translated as "Almighty."

# CONNECTING TO THE NAME

1. Why do you think God linked this particular name to the covenant he made with Abraham and his descendants?

2. In addition to revealing his name, God also changed Abram's and Sarai's names. What do their new names signify? See also Genesis 12:2–3.

3. What was Abraham's response to the revelation of God's name? How might you have responded if God had revealed himself to you as he did to Abraham?

4. List the promises God made to Abraham. What was Abraham's response to this incredible news?

5. Have you ever had to wait a long time before *El Shadday* acted in your circumstances? Describe your experience and how prolonged waiting tested your understanding of God.

6. What does the name *El Shadday*, God Almighty, mean to you? How have you experienced God's almighty power working on your behalf?

# PRAYING A PASSAGE WITH GOD'S NAME

Praise God because it is his nature to bless those who love. Spend a few moments reflecting on **EL SHADDAY**, God Almighty, as you read Genesis 49:22–26.

[22] "***Joseph*** is a fruitful tree,
    a fruitful tree by a spring,
        with branches climbing over a wall.
[23] Archers provoked him,
    shot at him,
        and attacked him.
[24] But his bow stayed steady, and his arms remained limber
    because of the help of the Mighty One of Jacob,
    because of the name of the Shepherd, the Rock of Israel,
[25] because of the ***El*** of your father who helps you,
    because of the ***Shadday*** who gives you
        blessings from the heavens above,
        blessings from the deep springs below the ground,
        blessings from breasts and womb.
[26] The blessings of your father are greater than
    the blessings of the oldest mountains
        and the riches of the ancient hills.
May these blessings rest on the head of Joseph,
    on the crown of the prince among his brothers.

## PRAYING THE NAME **EL SHADDAY** FOR MYSELF

Look up and read: Psalm 91:1–2, 14

This Psalm gives us a dialogue between the psalmist and God. The psalmist says, "I will say of the LORD, 'He is my refuge and my fortress (NIV)." What do you say about God? Read God's response to the psalmist in verse 14 and write out your own dialogue. What do you have to say to *El Shadday*?

_____

_____

_____

_____

_____

## PROMISES OF **EL SHADDAY**

²I will make you a great nation,
I will bless you.
I will make your name great,
    and you will be a blessing.
³I will bless those who bless you,
    and whoever curses you, I will curse.
        Through you every family on earth will be blessed."

—Genesis 12:2-3

## FOR DEEPER STUDY

*Read the following passages, considering the name* **EL SHADDAY** *and how its meaning relates to the context of the passage.*

Genesis 28:3            Ruth 1:20–22            Job 6:1–4, 13–14

# THE EVER-LASTING GOD OR THE ETERNAL GOD

## אֵל עוֹלָם
## EL OLAM

**El Olam** is the Hebrew name for the God who has no beginning and no end, the God for whom one day is like a thousand years and a thousand years are like one day. His plans stand firm forever, plans to give you a future full of hope. When you pray to the Everlasting God, you are praying to the God whose Son is called the Alpha and the Omega, the beginning and the end. He is the God whose love endures forever.

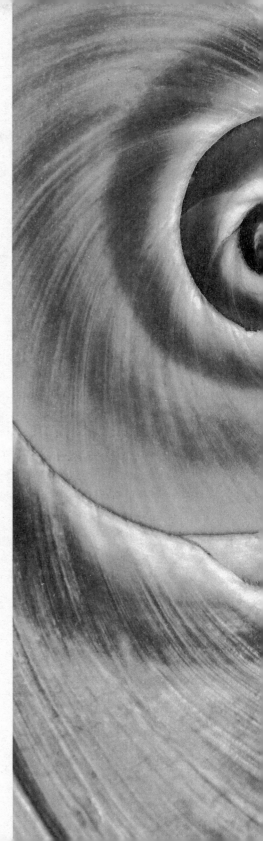

## KEY SCRIPTURE

"After they made the treaty at Beersheba, Abimelech and Phicol, the commander of his army, left and went back to the land of the Philistines. Abraham planted a tamarisk tree at Beersheba and worshiped **Yahweh, El Olam**, there."

—Genesis 21:32–33

# GOD REVEALS HIS NAME IN SCRIPTURE
## GENESIS 21:22–32

*Open your personal Bible translation and read the same passage. Make note to yourself when* **EL OLAM** *is used as God's name.*

22 At that time Abimelech, accompanied by Phicol, the commander of his army, said to Abraham, "**Elohim** is with you in everything you do. 23 Now, swear an oath to me here in front of **Elohim** that you will never cheat me, my children, or my descendants. Show me and the land where you've been living the same kindness that I have shown you."

24 Abraham said, "I so swear."

25 Then Abraham complained to Abimelech about a well which Abimelech's servants had seized. 26 Abimelech replied, "I don't know who did this. You didn't tell me, and I didn't hear about it until today."

27 Abraham took some sheep and cattle and gave them to Abimelech, and the two of them made an agreement. 28 Then Abraham set apart seven female lambs from the flock. 29 Abimelech asked him, "What is the meaning of these seven female lambs you have set apart?"

30 Abraham answered, "Accept these lambs from me so that they may be proof[a] that I dug this well." 31 This is why that place is called Beersheba,[b] because both of them swore an oath there.

32 After they made the treaty at Beersheba, Abimelech and Phicol, the commander of his army, left and went back to the land of the Philistines. 33 Abraham planted a tamarisk tree at Beersheba and worshiped **Yahweh**, **El Olam**, there. 34 Abraham lived a long time in the land of the Philistines.

## UNDERSTANDING THE NAME

Olam is a Hebrew word that occurs more than four hundred times in the Hebrew Scriptures. It is translated as "eternal," "everlasting," "forever," "lasting," "ever," or "ancient." It refers to the fullness of the experience of time or space. The title **El Olam** (EL o-LAM), meaning "Eternal God" or "Everlasting God," appears only four times. The word is applied to God and his laws, promises, covenant, and kingdom.

## CONNECTING TO THE NAME

1. Abimelech was the leader of the Philistines. What do his words say about the obvious nature of God's faithfulness to Abraham?

2. Beersheba means "well of the oath." Why do you think Abraham planted a tamarisk (a relatively long-living tree requiring large amounts of water and producing as many as 500,000 seeds per plant) after the two men swore an oath about Abraham's well?

3. What images come to mind when you think of El Olam, "Eternal God" or "Everlasting God"?

4. What might these names imply about the nature of God's promises?

# PRAYING A PASSAGE WITH GOD'S NAME

Praise God for his eternal vitality. Spend a few moments reflecting on the name **El Olam**, the Everlasting God, as you read Isaiah 40:28–29.

> <sup>28</sup> Don't you know?
>> Haven't you heard?
>> **El Olam, Yahweh**, the Creator of the ends of the
>>> earth,
>> doesn't grow tired or become weary.
>>> His understanding is beyond reach.
> <sup>29</sup> He gives strength to those who grow tired
>> and increases the strength of those who are weak.

## PRAYING THE NAME EL OLAM FOR MYSELF

*Look up and read: Psalm 90:4, 10, 12*

What are you waiting for? Do you believe that God knows the desires of your heart and is patiently listening to your prayers? Write two lists—a list of things you have waited for and how long it took for your prayers to be answered, and a list of things that you are still waiting on. With the Psalmist, ask **El Olam** to teach you to number your days.

| | |
| --- | --- |
| | |
| | |
| | |
| | |

## PROMISES FROM **EL OLAM**

*"**Yahweh's** plan stands firm forever.*
His thoughts stand firm in every generation."

—Psalm 33:11

### FOR DEEPER STUDY

*Read the following passages, considering the name* **EL OLAM** *and how its meaning relates to the context of the passage.*

Psalms 33:11; 90; 100; 103:13–18; 145:13

Ecclesiastes 3:11

Isaiah 40:28–31; 46:3–4

John 6:40

Revelation 1:4–8

WEEK 5

# THE LORD WILL PROVIDE

## יהוה יִרְאֶה
## *YAHWEH YIREH*

The Hebrew verb ra'ah (from which yireh is derived) means "to see." In this case, it is translated as "provide." Since God sees the future as well as the past and the present, he is able to anticipate and provide for what is needed. Interestingly the English word "provision" is made up of two Latin words that mean "to see beforehand." When you pray to **Yahweh Yireh**, you are praying to the God who sees the situation beforehand and is able to provide for your needs.

## KEY SCRIPTURE

When Abraham looked around, he saw a ram behind him caught by its horns in a bush. So Abraham took the ram and sacrificed it as a burnt offering in place of his son. Abraham named that place **Yahweh Yireh**. It is still said today, "On the mountain of **Yahweh** it will be provided."

—Genesis 22:13–14

# GOD REVEALS HIS NAME IN SCRIPTURE
## GENESIS 22:1–14

*Open your personal Bible translation and read the same passage. Make note to yourself or using a simple mark in your Bible when the name* **YAHWEH YIREH** *is used.*

Later **Elohim** tested Abraham and called to him, "Abraham!"

"Yes, here I am!" he answered.

[2] **Elohim** said, "Take your son, your only son Isaac, whom you love, and go to Moriah. Sacrifice him there as a burnt offering on one of the mountains that I will show you."

[3] Early the next morning Abraham saddled his donkey. He took with him two of his servants and his son Isaac. When he had cut the wood for the burnt offering, he set out for the place that **Elohim** had told him about. [4] Two days later Abraham saw the place in the distance. [5] Then Abraham said to his servants, "You stay here with the donkey while the boy and I go over there. We'll worship. After that we'll come back to you."

[6] Then Abraham took the wood for the burnt offering and gave it to his son Isaac. Abraham carried the burning coals and the knife. The two of them went on together.

[7] Isaac spoke up and said, "Father?"

"Yes, Son?" Abraham answered.

Isaac asked, "We have the burning coals and the wood, but where is the lamb for the burnt offering?"

[8] Abraham answered, "**Elohim** will provide a lamb for the burnt offering, Son."

The two of them went on together. [9] When they came to the place that **Elohim** had told him about, Abraham built the altar and arranged the wood on it. Then he tied up his son Isaac and laid him on top of the wood on the altar. [10] Next, Abraham picked up the knife and took it in his hand to sacrifice his son. [11] But the Messenger of **Yahweh** called to him from heaven and said, "Abraham! Abraham!"

"Yes?" he answered.

¹² "Do not lay a hand on the boy," he said. "Do not do anything to him. Now I know that you fear **Elohim**, because you did not refuse to give me your son, your only son."

¹³ When Abraham looked around, he saw a ram behind him caught by its horns in a bush. So Abraham took the ram and sacrificed it as a burnt offering in place of his son. ¹⁴ Abraham named that place **Yahweh Yireh**. It is still said today, "On the mountain of **Yahweh** it will be provided."

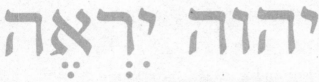

## UNDERSTANDING THE NAME

Moriah, the site of Abraham's thwarted attempt to sacrifice his son, has been traditionally associated with the temple mount in Jerusalem. Though scholars debate the location it is interesting to note that the traditional location is today occupied by a Muslim shrine called the Dome of the Rock. Jesus, whom John the Baptist called "the Lamb of God," is thought to have been crucified just a quarter mile away from Mount Moriah. It was there that Yahweh Yireh (yah-WEH yir-EH) provided the one sacrifice that would make our peace with him.

## CONNECTING TO THE NAME

1. Imagine that you are Abraham, making the three-day trip toward Moriah to sacrifice your son. What is in your heart?

2. Compare the scene in which a ram is sacrificed in Isaac's place in this passage to John 1:29: "The next day John [the Baptist] saw Jesus coming toward him and said, 'Look, the Lamb of God, who takes away the sin of the world!' " (NIV)

3. Why do you think God tests people?

4. Notice how Abraham had first to obey God in order to see God's provision. How has obedience affected your experience of God's provision?

5. What is the most difficult sacrifice the Lord has asked you to make? How did you respond?

6. In what ways has *Yahweh Yireh* provided for you? Think about the last week, the last month, the last year.

## PRAYING A PASSAGE WITH GOD'S NAME

Thank God for the blessings you have received because of Abraham's obedience. Spend a few moments reflecting on the name **Yahweh Yireh** as you read Genesis 22:16–18.

> "I am taking an oath on my own name, declares **Yahweh**, that because you have done this and have not refused to give me your son, your only son, [17] I will certainly bless you and make your descendants as numerous as the stars in the sky and the grains of sand on the seashore. Your descendants will take possession of their enemies' cities. [18] Through your descendant all the nations of the earth will be blessed, because you have obeyed me."

## PRAYING THE NAME **YAHWEH YIREH** FOR MYSELF

Look up and read: Genesis 22:9–12

When God asked Abraham to sacrifice Isaac, He was asking for the most precious thing that Abraham had. Sometimes, we withhold the things closest to our heart from God, because we don't trust his plan for them. Ask God to give you understanding. Are you holding back anything from *Yahweh Yireh*?

_____

_____

_____

_____

_____

## PROMISES FROM **YAHWEH YIREH**

[12] So, people who think they are standing firmly should be careful that they don't fall.

[13] There isn't any temptation that you have experienced which is unusual for humans. God, who faithfully keeps his promises, will not allow you to be tempted beyond your power to resist. But when you are tempted, he will also give you the ability to endure the temptation as your way of escape.

—1 Corinthians 10:12–13

## FOR DEEPER STUDY

*Read the following passages, considering the name* **YAHWEH YIREH** *and how its meaning relates to the context of the passage.*

Deuteronomy 15:4–6          Matthew 6:25–33          John 3:16

Romans 8:32          1 Timothy 6:17–19

# LORD

## יהוה
## YAHWEH

The name **Yahweh** occurs more than 6,800 times in the Old Testament. It appears in every book but Esther, Ecclesiastes, and the Song of Songs. As the sacred, personal name of Israel's God, it was eventually spoken aloud only by priests worshiping in the Jerusalem temple. After the destruction of the temple in AD 70, the name was not pronounced at all. *Adonay* was substituted for **Yahweh** whenever it appeared in the biblical text. Because of this, the correct pronunciation of this name was eventually lost. English editions of the Bible usually translate *Adonay* as "Lord" and **Yahweh** as "LORD." **Yahweh** is the name that is most closely linked to God's redeeming acts in the history of his chosen people. We know God because of what he has done. When you pray to *Yahweh*, remember that he is the same God who draws near to save you from the tyranny of sin just as he saved his people from slavery in Egypt.

## KEY SCRIPTURE

*Elohim* answered Moses, "*Ehyeh* Who *Ehyeh* [I AM WHO I AM]. This is what you must say to the people of Israel: '*Ehyeh* [I AM] has sent me to you.'"

Again *Elohim* said to Moses, "This is what you must say to the people of Israel: *Yahweh Elohim* [THE LORD] of your ancestors, the *Elohim* [LORD] of Abraham, Isaac, and Jacob, has sent me to you. This is my name forever. This is my title throughout every generation.

—Exodus 3:14–15

# GOD REVEALS HIS NAME IN SCRIPTURE
## EXODUS 3:1–3, 6–8, 10–20

*Open your personal Bible translation and read the same passage. Make note to yourself or using a simple mark in your Bible every time* **YAHWEH** *is the name God uses for himself.*

Moses was taking care of the sheep of his father-in-law Jethro, the priest of Midian. As he led the sheep to the far side of the desert, he came to Horeb, the mountain of *Elohim*.

[2] The Messenger of *Yahweh* appeared to him there as flames of fire coming out of a bush. Moses looked, and although the bush was on fire, it was not burning up. [3] So he thought, "Why isn't this bush burning up? I must go over there and see this strange sight."

[6] I am the *Elohim* of your ancestors,[a] the *Elohim* of Abraham, Isaac, and Jacob." Moses hid his face because he was afraid to look at *Elohim*.

[7] *Yahweh* said, "I have seen the misery of my people in Egypt, and I have heard them crying out because of the slave drivers. I know how much they're suffering. [8] I have come to rescue them from the power of the Egyptians and to bring them from that land to a good land with plenty of room for everyone. It is a land flowing with milk and honey where the Canaanites, Hittites, Amorites, Perizzites, Hivites, and Jebusites live.

[10] Now, go! I am sending you to Pharaoh so that you can bring my people Israel out of Egypt."

[11] But Moses said to *Elohim*, "Who am I that I should go to Pharaoh and bring the people of Israel out of Egypt?"

[12] *Elohim* answered, "I will be with you. And this will be the proof that I sent you: When you bring the people out of Egypt, all of you

will worship **Elohim** on this mountain."

[13] Then Moses replied to **Elohim**, "Suppose I go to the people of Israel and say to them, 'The **Elohim** of your ancestors has sent me to you,' and they ask me, 'What is his name?' What should I tell them?"

[14] **Elohim** answered Moses, "**Ehyeh** Who **Ehyeh** [I AM WHO I AM]. This is what you must say to the people of Israel: '**Ehyeh** [I AM]. has sent me to you.'"

[15] Again **Elohim** said to Moses, "This is what you must say to the people of Israel: **Yahweh Elohim** of your ancestors, the **Elohim** of Abraham, Isaac, and Jacob, has sent me to you. This is my name forever. This is my title throughout every generation.

[16] "Go, assemble the leaders of Israel. Say to them, '**Yahweh Elohim** of your ancestors, the **Elohim** of Abraham, Isaac, and Jacob, appeared to me. He said, "I have paid close attention to you and have seen what has been done to you in Egypt. [17] I promise I will take you away from your misery in Egypt to the land of the Canaanites, Hittites, Amorites, Perizzites, Hivites, and Jebusites, a land flowing with milk and honey."'

[18] "The leaders of Israel will listen to you. Then you and the leaders must go to the king of Egypt and say to him, '**Yahweh Elohim** of the Hebrews has met with us. Please let us travel three days into the desert to offer sacrifices to **Yahweh** our **Elohim**.' [19] I know that the king of Egypt will not let you go, even if he is forced to. [20] So I will use my power to strike Egypt. After all the miracles that I will do there, he will let you go.

## UNDERSTANDING THE NAME

Afraid of profaning this covenant name of God, various rabbinical writers spoke of it as "The Name," "The Great and Terrible Name," "The Unutterable Name," "The Ineffable Name," "The Holy Name," and "The Distinguished Name." Also known as the Tetragrammaton, because it is formed by the four Hebrew consonants YHWH (JHVH in German), it was first rendered Jehovah in the Middle Ages and enshrined as such in the King James Version of the Bible (Exodus 6:3; Psalm 83:18; Isaiah 12:2; 26:4). This mispronunciation arose when in the tenth century Jewish scholars began supplying vowels to Hebrew words, which had formerly been written without them. Since **Adonay** was always substituted for **Yahweh** (pronounced yah-WEH, as scholars now think) in the biblical text, the Hebrew vowels for Adonay were inserted into the four letters of the Tetragrammaton: YaHoWaH.

Unfortunately, the translation "LORD," which is a title rather than a name, obscures the personal nature of this name for God. Though the meaning of Yahweh is disputed, the mysterious self-description in Exodus 3:14, "I AM WHO I AM," may convey the sense not only that God is self-existent but that he is always present with his people. Yahweh is not a God who is remote or aloof but one who is always near, intervening in history on behalf of his people. The knowledge of God's proper name implies a covenant relationship. God's covenant name is closely associated with his saving acts in Exodus. The name Yahweh evokes images of God's saving power in the lives of his people.

## CONNECTING TO THE NAME

1. Why do you think Moses asked God to reveal his name?

2. Make a list of everything God has revealed about himself in this passage.

3. What does this passage reveal about what was in the heart of God in regard to his people?

4. What was the catalyst for God's action?

5. Why do you think Moses was afraid to look at God?

6. Moses' reluctance to do what God was asking is not hard to understand. Describe a time when you were similarly reluctant to do something you thought God was calling you to do.

## PRAYING A PASSAGE WITH GOD'S NAME

As you thank God for his goodness, ask him to break any false images of him that you may have developed. Spend a few moments reflecting on the name **Yahweh**, your LORD, as you read Psalm 103:1–5.

> Praise **Yahweh**, my soul!
>> Praise his holy name, all that is within me.
> ² Praise **Yahweh**, my soul,
>> and never forget all the good he has done:
>>> ³ He is the one who forgives all your sins,
>>>> the one who heals all your diseases,
>>>>> ⁴ the one who rescues your life from the pit,
>>>>> the one who crowns you with mercy and
>>>>>> compassion,
>>>>> ⁵ the one who fills your life with blessings
>>>>>> so that you become young again like an
>>>>>> eagle.

## PRAYING THE NAME **YAHWEH** FOR MYSELF

Look up and read: Exodus 20:2–3

God asks you to worship Him alone. This commandment doesn't restrict freedom; it gains the only real freedom there is, the freedom to worship God. How has giving your life to Him made you a freer person? Ask God to show you how you have been taken from bondage to freedom.

_____

_____

_____

_____

## PROMISES FROM **YAHWEH**

**Yahweh** will be your confidence.
    He will keep your foot from getting caught.
    —Proverbs 3:26

**Yahweh** is near to those whose hearts are humble. He saves
    those whose spirits are crushed.
    —Psalm 34:18

## FOR DEEPER STUDY

*Read the following passages, considering the name* **YAHWEH** *and how its meaning relates to the context of the passage.*

Exodus 34:4–7          Numbers 6:24–27          Deuteronomy 28:9–13

Psalms 32:10; 34:4–20; 37:34–40; 103

# LORD, MASTER

## אֲדֹנָי
### ADONAY

*Adonay* is a Hebrew word meaning "Lord," a name that implies relationship: God is Lord, and we are his servants. As a word referring to God it appears more than three hundred times in the Hebrew Scriptures. As you pray to **Adonay**, tell him you want to surrender every aspect of your life to him. Pray for the grace to become the kind of servant who is quick to do God's will. Remember, too, that the Lord is the only one who can empower you to fulfill his purpose for your life. In fact, it is in knowing him as your Lord that you will discover a true sense of purpose. The New Testament depicts Jesus as both Lord and Servant. In this latter role he exemplifies what our relationship to **Adonay** is to be.

## KEY SCRIPTURE

I said to *Yahweh*, "You are my ***Adonay***. Without you, I have nothing good."

—Psalm 16:2

# GOD REVEALS HIS NAME IN SCRIPTURE
## EXODUS 4:1–5, 10–15

*Open your personal Bible translation and read the same passage. Make note where* **ADONAY** *is used as God's name.*

"They will never believe me or listen to me!" Moses protested. "They will say, '*Yahweh* didn't appear to you.'"

[2] Then *Yahweh* asked him, "What's that in your hand?"

He answered, "A shepherd's staff."

[3] *Yahweh* said, "Throw it on the ground."

When Moses threw it on the ground, it became a snake, and he ran away from it.

[4] Then *Yahweh* said to Moses, "Reach out and grab the snake by its tail." He reached out and grabbed it, and it turned back into a staff as he held it. [5] The LORD explained, "This is to convince the people that ***Yahweh Elohim*** of their ancestors, the ***Elohim*** of Abraham, Isaac, and Jacob, appeared to you."

[10] Moses said to *Yahweh*, "Please, ***Adonay***, I'm not a good speaker. I've never been a good speaker, and I'm not now, even though you've spoken to me. I speak slowly, and I become tongue-tied easily."

[11] *Yahweh* asked him, "Who gave humans their mouths? Who makes humans unable to talk or hear? Who gives them sight or makes them blind? It is I, *Yahweh*! [12] Now go, and I will help you speak and will teach you what to say."

[13] But Moses said, "Please, ***Adonay***, send someone else."

[14] Then *Yahweh* became angry with Moses and asked, "What about your brother Aaron the Levite? I know he can speak well. He's already on his way to meet you, and he will be very glad to see you. [15] You will speak to him and tell him what to say. I will help both of you speak, and I will teach you both what to do.

## UNDERSTANDING THE NAME

**Adon** is a Hebrew word that means "lord" in the sense of an owner, master, or superior. It is frequently used as a term of respect and always refers to people. **Adonay** (a-do-NAI) is the plural form of **adon** and always refers to God as Lord or Master. In the Old Testament it is rendered as "Lord" (distinct from "LORD," the rendering for the Hebrew name **Yahweh**). When **Adonay** and **Yahweh** appear together, the NIV renders the name as "Sovereign LORD," while older translations of the Bible render it "LORD God." **Adonay** is first used in Genesis 15:2. In the New Testament, the Greek word most often translated "Lord" is **Kyrios**.

## CONNECTING TO THE NAME

1. How is the lordship of God displayed in Exodus 4? (Note that Pharaoh's headdress included a metal cobra, symbolizing his sovereignty.)

2. Imagine what Moses thought might happen to him if he obeyed *Adonay*? When might you have had similar fears about obeying the Lord?

3. Why was the Lord angry with Moses?

4. Notice that Moses expressed reluctance to doing God's will at the same time he was addressing him as "Lord." Have you ever done the same? What held you back from doing what *Adonay* was asking?

5. Although God was angry with Moses, how did he respond to Moses' request to send someone else?

6. Has God ever sent someone to come alongside you when you were insecure and hesitant about obeying? Describe how this person helped you.

## PRAYING A PASSAGE WITH GOD'S NAME

*Ask God to show you the connection between his lordship and his blessings. Thank him for every blessing you can think of and spend a few moments reflecting on the name **Adonay**, Lord, as you read Psalm 16:2 and 73:25–26.*

> I said to **Yahweh**,
>> "You are my **Adonay**. Without you, I have nothing good."
>
> As long as I have you,
>> I don't need anyone else in heaven or on earth.
> 26 My body and mind may waste away,
>> but **Elohim** remains the foundation of my life
>> and my inheritance forever.

## PRAYING THE NAME **ADONAY** FOR MYSELF

Look up and read: Nehemiah 4:7–18

The prophet Nehemiah assures us in Nehemiah 4:14, "Don't be afraid of our enemies." Ask God to reveal to you any fears that you have that are holding you back from his service. Write these down and pray with them, remembering that he is your **Adonay,** and that he will fight with you and for you.

_____

_____

_____

_____

## PROMISES FROM **ADONAY**

[11] **_Elohim_** has spoken once.
   I have heard it said twice:
      "Power belongs to **_Elohim_**.
[12] Mercy belongs to you, O **_Adonay_**.
   You reward a person based on what he has done."
   —Psalm 62:11–12

But you, O **_Adonay_**, are a compassionate and merciful God.
   You are patient, always faithful and ready to forgive.
   —Psalm 86:15

## FOR DEEPER STUDY

_Read the following passages, considering the name_ **ADONAY** _and how its meaning relates to the context of the passage._

Psalms 16:2; 54:4; 62:11–12; 86:15; 136:3        Isaiah 6:1–8

Daniel 9:17–19        Luke 17:7–10        Philippians 2:5–11

# THE LORD WHO HEALS

## יהוה רפֶה
### *YAHWEH ROPHE*

The Hebrew word rophe means "heal," "cure," "restore," or "make whole." Shortly after his people left Egypt for the Promised Land, God revealed himself as **Yahweh Rophe**, "the Lord who heals." The Hebrew Scriptures indicate that God is the source of all healing. As you pray to **Yahweh Rophe**, ask him to search your heart. Take time to let him show you what it contains. If he uncovers any sin, ask for his forgiveness and then pray for healing. The New Testament reveals Jesus as the Great Physician, the healer of body and soul, whose miracles point to the kingdom of God.

## KEY SCRIPTURE

He said, "If you will listen carefully to **Yahweh** your **Elohim** and do what he considers right, if you pay attention to his commands and obey all his laws, I will never make you suffer any of the diseases I made the Egyptians suffer, because I am **Yahweh Ropheka**."

—Exodus 15:26

# GOD REVEALS HIS NAME IN SCRIPTURE
## EXODUS 15: 20–27

*Open your personal Bible translation and read the same passage. Make note to yourself or using a simple mark in your Bible every time Yahweh Rophe* **YAHWEH ROPHE** *is the name God uses for himself.*

[20] Then the prophet Miriam, Aaron's sister, took a tambourine in her hand. All the women, dancing with tambourines, followed her. [21] Miriam sang to them:

"Sing to **Yahweh**.

He has won a glorious victory.

He has thrown horses and their riders into the sea."

[22] Moses led Israel away from the Red Sea into the desert of Shur. For three days they traveled in the desert without finding water. [23] When they came to Marah, they couldn't drink the water because it tasted bitter. That's why the place was called Marah [Bitter Place]. [24] The people complained about Moses by asking, "What are we supposed to drink?"

[25] Moses cried out to **Yahweh**, and **Yahweh** showed[a] him a piece of wood. He threw it into the water, and the water became sweet.

There **Yahweh** set down laws and rules for them to live by, and there he tested them. [26] He said, "If you will listen carefully to **Yahweh** your **Elohim** and do what he considers right, if you pay attention to his commands and obey all his laws, I will never make you suffer any of the diseases I made the Egyptians suffer, because I am **Yahweh Ropheka**."

[27] Next, they went to Elim, where there were 12 springs and 70 palm trees. They camped there by the water.

## UNDERSTANDING THE NAME

The verb from which Rophe is derived occurs sixty-seven times in the Old Testament. Though it often refers to physical healing, it usually has a larger meaning as well, involving the entire person. Rather than merely healing the body, Yahweh Rophe (yah-WEH ro-FEH) heals the mind and soul as well. This Hebrew verb is also used in other ways—for example, God "heals" water, land, and nations, and he "repairs" an altar. Significantly, God also heals sin and apostasy. The Hebrew Scriptures, in fact, link sickness and sin by presenting sin as the cause of illness just as it is the cause of death. In the New Testament, the corresponding Greek word is iaomai, which can refer to deliverance from death, demons, sickness, and sin.

Jesus, the great healer, clearly indicated that sickness is not necessarily caused by sin on the part of the person who is ill. Rather, it can result from living in a sinful, fallen world.

## CONNECTING TO THE NAME

1. How did circumstances influence the people's attitude toward God? Describe times in your own life when your circumstances have caused your attitude toward God to fluctuate.

2. How did Moses react to the circumstances? What does his example teach about how we should respond to difficult circumstances?

3. The waters of Marah were bitter and God made them sweet. What areas of bitterness in your life have been healed or might still need healing?

4. On what condition does God base his promise to keep the Israelites from disease?

5. Describe a time in your life when breaking *Yahweh Rophe's* commands caused you suffering or even sickness.

6. God tested the Israelites with adverse circumstances, thus uncovering what was in their hearts. Describe ways in which you have experienced God testing you. How did you respond?

7. What does this passage say about God's control over sickness and health?

8. How have you experienced God answering your own prayers for healing?

# PRAYING A PASSAGE WITH GOD'S NAME

Praise God for the surprising way in which he has healed our sin, healing us through the wounds of his son. Spend a few moments reflecting on the name **Yahweh Rophe**, The LORD Who Heals, as you read Isaiah 53:4–5.

> He certainly has taken upon himself our suffering
>   and carried our sorrows,
>     but we thought that **Elohim** had wounded him,
>       beat him, and punished him.
> He was wounded for our rebellious acts.
>   He was crushed for our sins.
>     He was punished so that we could have peace,
>       and we received healing from his wounds.

## PRAYING THE NAME **YAHWEH ROPHE** FOR MYSELF

Look up and read: Isaiah 38:16–17

Do you feel the pressure to live by a list of rules? This is not what God wants for you. He wants you to be drawn by his grace and by the great care he put into his Word. The law found in the Bible was written by Yahweh Rophe, the only One who can truly heal your heart. Ask God to show you where the pressure you feel is truly coming from.

_____

_____

_____

_____

## PROMISES FROM **YAHWEH ROPHE**

This is what **Yahweh Elohim** of your ancestor David says: I've heard your prayer. I've seen your tears. Now I'm going to heal you.

—2 Kings 20:5

When **Yeshua** heard this, he told the synagogue leader, "Don't be afraid! Just believe, and she will get well."

—Luke 8:50

### FOR DEEPER STUDY

*Read the following passages, considering the name* **YAHWEH ROPHE** *and how its meaning relates to the context of the passage.*

Psalms 38; 103:1–5; 147:1–6

Isaiah 53; 57:18–20

Jeremiah 17:14

Matthew 8:16–17

Luke 4:14–19; 8:50

John 9:1–7

James 5:14–16

# THE LORD MY BANNER

## יהוה נִסִּי
### *YAHWEH NISSI*

Ancient armies carried standards or banners that served as marks of identification and as symbols that embodied the ideals of a people. A banner, like a flag, was something that could be seen from afar, serving as a rallying point for troops before a battle. We know that banners were used in Egypt, Babylonia, Assyria, and Persia, and the Israelites apparently carried them on their march through the desert. When you pray to *Yahweh Nissi,* you are praying to the God who is powerful enough to overcome any foe.

## KEY SCRIPTURE

[15] Moses built an altar and called it **Yahweh Nissi**. [16] He said, "Because a hand was lifted against **Yah's** throne, **Yahweh** will be at war against the Amalekites from one generation to the next."

—Exodus 17:15-16

# GOD REVEALS HIS NAME IN SCRIPTURE
## EXODUS 17:8–16

*Open your personal Bible translation and read the same passage. Make note where* **YAHWEH NISSI** *is used as God's name.*

[8] The Amalekites fought Israel at Rephidim. [9] Moses said to Joshua, "Choose some of our men. Then fight the Amalekites. Tomorrow I will stand on top of the hill. I will hold in my hand the staff **Elohim** told me to take along."

[10] Joshua did as Moses told him and fought the Amalekites, while Moses, Aaron, and Hur went to the top of the hill. [11] As long as Moses held up his hands, Israel would win, but as soon as he put his hands down, the Amalekites would start to win. [12] Eventually, Moses' hands felt heavy. So Aaron and Hur took a rock, put it under him, and he sat on it. Aaron held up one hand, and Hur held up the other. His hands remained steady until sunset. [13] So Joshua defeated the Amalekite army in battle.

[14] **Yahweh** said to Moses, "Write this reminder on a scroll, and make sure that Joshua hears it, too: I will completely erase any memory of the Amalekites from the earth."

[15] Moses built an altar and called it **Yahweh Nissi**. [16] He said, "Because a hand was lifted against **Yah's** throne, **Yahweh** will be at war against the Amalekites from one generation to the next."

## UNDERSTANDING THE NAME

Unlike fabric flags, ancient banners were usually made out of wood or metal and shaped into various figures or emblems that could be fastened to a bare staff or a long pole. Depicting birds, animals, or gods, they often glistened brightly in the sun so that they could be seen from far off. A banner carried at the head of an army or planted on a high hill served as a rallying point for troops before battle or as an announcement of a victory already won.

Because banners embodied the ideals and aspirations of whoever carried them, they aroused devotion to a nation, a cause, or a leader. When Moses held up the staff of God in the battle with the Amale kites, he was holding it like a banner, appealing to God's power. By building an altar and naming it *Yahweh Nissi* (yah-WEH nis-SEE), "The Lord is my Banner," he created a memorial of God's protection and power during the Israelites' first battle after leaving Egypt.

## CONNECTING TO THE NAME

1. The Amalekites were fierce enemies of the Israelites and the first to attack them after their liberation from Egypt (see Deuteronomy 25:17–19). As members of God's people, we face spiritual enemies intent on destroying God's plans and purposes for our lives. What are some of the enemies you face and how have you dealt with them?

2. What does it mean to engage in spiritual battles today? What difference would it make if you could say, like Moses, "The Lord is my Banner"?

3. Aaron and Hur helped Moses when he grew weary of holding up his hands. Has *Yahweh Nissi* ever sent others to help you in the midst of battle? Who and how?

4. What battles might you be trying to fight in your own strength?

5. How is Jesus God's banner of victory for us?

6. How might lifting high the cross of Christ help you to overcome?

## PRAYING A PASSAGE WITH GOD'S NAME

Praise God for his power to save the children in your life. Spend time asking God to rescue and deliver them. Focus on the name **Yahweh Nissi**, the LORD My Banner, as you read Isaiah 49:22–23.

> I will lift my hand to signal the nations.
>> I will raise my flag for the people.
>> They will bring your sons in their arms
>>> and carry your daughters on their shoulders.
> 23 Then kings will be your foster fathers,
>> and their queens will nurse you.
>> They will bow in front of you
>>> with their faces touching the ground.
> They will lick the dust at your feet.
>> Then you will know that I am **Yahweh**.
>>> Those who wait with hope for me will not be put to shame.

## PRAYING THE NAME **YAHWEH NISSI** FOR MYSELF

Look up and read Numbers 21:8–9

Moses was told by God to make a bronze snake and place it on a pole–any Israelite bitten by a poisonous snake could look at the bronze snake and live. Where is the first place you look when you are suffering? Do you immediately look to *Yahweh Nissi*, or is your heart attracted elsewhere?

_____

_____

_____

_____

# PROMISES FROM **YAHWEH NISSI**

[4] Yet, you have raised a flag for those who fear you
    so that they can rally to it
        when attacked by bows and arrows. *Selah*
—Psalm 60:4

## FOR DEEPER STUDY

*Read the following passages, considering the name* **YAHWEH NISSI** *and how its meaning relates to the context of the passage.*

Psalms 20; 60:4        Song of Songs 2:4        Isaiah 11:10–12; 49:22–25

John 3:14–15        1 Corinthians 1:18

# CONSUMING FIRE, JEALOUS GOD

## אֵשׁ אֹכְלָה, אֵל קַנָּה

### ESH OKLAH, EL KANNA

The Lord is a Consuming Fire who will ultimately destroy whatever is opposed to his holiness. He is also a Jealous God, who loves us completely and who, therefore, demands our wholehearted response. If we love him, we can be confident of his mercy, and our own zeal will make us jealous for God's honor and glory. When you pray the names of Esh Oklah and El Kanna, ask God to give you and the church a deeper understanding of his holiness and a greater desire to honor and exalt his name.

## KEY SCRIPTURES

Never worship any other god, because **Yahweh** is **El Kanna**. In fact, he is known for not tolerating rivals.

—Exodus 34:14

Be careful that you don't forget the promise that **Yahweh** your **Elohim** made to you. Don't make your own carved idols or statues that represent anything **Yahweh** your **Elohim** has forbidden. **Yahweh** your **Elohim** is **Esh Oklah**, **El Kanna**.

—Deuteronomy 4:23–24

# GOD REVEALS HIS NAME IN SCRIPTURE
## EXODUS 34:10–14; DEUTERONOMY 4:23–24; DEUTERONOMY 6:13–19

*Open your personal Bible translation and read these passages. Make a note where **EL KANNA** or **ESH OKLAH** is used as God's name.*

Ex 34:10 **Yahweh** said, "I'm making my promise again. In front of all your people I will perform miracles that have never been done in any other nation in all the world. All the people around you will see how awesome these miracles are that I will perform for you. ¹¹Do everything that I command today. Then I will force the Amorites, Canaanites, Hittites, Perizzites, Hivites, and Jebusites out of your way. ¹²Be careful not to make a treaty with those who live in the land where you're going. This will prove to be a trap to you. But tear down their altars, crush their sacred stones, and cut down their poles dedicated to the goddess Asherah. ¹⁴(Never worship any other god, because **Yahweh** is **El Kanna**. In fact, he is known for not tolerating rivals.)

Deut 4:23 Be careful that you don't forget the promise that **Yahweh** your **Elohim** made to you. Don't make your own carved idols or statues that represent anything **Yahweh** your **Elohim** has forbidden. ²⁴ **Yahweh** your **Elohim** is **Esh Oklah**, **El Kanna**.

6:13 You must fear **Yahweh** your **Elohim**, serve him, and take your oaths only in his name. Never worship any of the gods worshiped by the people around you. If you do, **Yahweh** your **Elohim** will become very angry with you and will wipe you off the face of the earth, because **Yahweh** your **Elohim**, who is with you, is **El Kanna**.

[16] Never test **Yahweh** your **Elohim** as you did at Massah. Be sure to obey the commands of **Yahweh** your **Elohim** and the regulations and laws he has given you. Do what **Yahweh** considers right and good. Then things will go well for you, and you will enter and take possession of that good land which **Yahweh** promised to your ancestors with an oath. You will see **Yahweh** expel your enemies as he said he would.

## UNDERSTANDING THE NAME

God sometimes manifested himself through images of fire—as a blazing torch, in the burning bush, or as a pillar of fire. When Moses met with God on Mount Sinai, the Israelites thought the glory of the Lord looked like a consuming fire on top of the mountain.

Most often, when Scripture pictures God as a consuming fire **Esh Oklah**; AISH o-KLAH, it is in connection with expressions of divine anger against the sins of human beings and nations. Even so, his jealousy is not the "green-eyed monster" so often associated with human jealousy. As biblical scholar Edward Mac pointed out: "This word . . . did not bear the evil meaning now associated with it in our usage, but rather signified 'righteous zeal,' Jehovah's zeal for His own name or glory."

Even so, Scripture compares God's jealousy to what a husband feels when his wife has been unfaithful. No wonder the first of the Ten Commandments prohibits the worship of other gods. The Lord is a Jealous God (**El Kanna**; EL kan-NAH), who cannot endure unfaith- fulness. Jesus expressed this same kind of exclusiveness when he told his disciples: "I am the way and the truth and the life. No one comes to the Father except through me. If you really knew me, you would know my Father as well. From now on, you do know him and have seen him" (John 14:6–7 NIV).

# CONNECTING TO THE NAME

1. What promises does God make in the Exodus passage?

2. What commands does God give in all three passages?

3. What warnings does he issue?

4. Why do you think the Lord said that his name is *El Kannah*, Jealous God?

5. What is the significance of this particular title of God in relation to his covenant?

6. How does this name of God relate to your own life? To the church today?

# PRAYING A PASSAGE WITH GOD'S NAME

Praise God for his jealous love for you and ask him for the grace to forsake any rivals that try to claim your allegiance. Focus on the name El Kanna, Jealous God, as you read Exodus 34:14.

> [14]Never worship any other God because Yahweh is *El Kanna*. In fact he is known for not tolerating rivals.

## PRAYING THE NAME **EL KANNA** FOR MYSELF

Look up and read: Hebrews 12:28–29

What do you think of when you think of "fire"? Have you ever sat and watched the flames of a fire leaping up in their intricate dance? Fire itself inspires a kind of reverence and stillness. How can you cultivate more reverence and awe towards *El Kanna*?

_____

_____

_____

_____

# PROMISES FROM **ESH OKLAH, EL KANNA**

> [23]Be careful that you don't forget the promise that **Yahweh** your **Elohim** made to you. Don't make your own carved idols or statues that represent anything **Yahweh** your **Elohim** has forbidden. [24]**Yahweh** your **Elohim** is **Esh Oklah, El Kanna**.
>
> —Deuteronomy 4:23-24

> [4]The sinners in Zion are terrified.
> Trembling seizes the ungodly.
> Can any of us live through a fire that destroys?
> Can any of us live through a fire that burns forever?
> [15]The person who does what is right and speaks the truth will live.
>
> —Isaiah 33:14-15

## FOR DEEPER STUDY

*Read the following passages, considering the names* **ESH OKLAH** *and* **EL KANNA** *and how its meaning relates to the context of the passage.*

Exodus 24:15

Deuteronomy 5:8–10

Psalm 18:6–19

Isaiah 33:14–15; 64:1–8

Daniel 3:1–25

Malachi 3:2–3

# HOLY ONE OF ISRAEL

## קְדוֹשׁ יִשְׂרָאֵל
### QEDOSH YISRAEL

The title "Holy One of Israel" emphasizes God's uniqueness, otherness, and mystery as well as his call to his people to become holy as he is. The Israelites were to be set apart for God, devoted to his service, and committed to honoring his character by reflecting it in all their relationships. In the New Testament Jesus was recognized as the Holy One of God by demons who were threatened by his power and purity. As believers, we are called to reflect the character of Christ, to be holy even as he is holy.

When you pray to the Holy One of Israel, you are praying to the God whose holiness not only encompasses his separation from evil, but his power, knowledge, justice, mercy, goodness, and love.

## KEY SCRIPTURE

**Yahweh** spoke to Moses, "Tell the whole congregation of Israel: Be holy because I, **Yahweh** your **Elohim**, am holy."

—Leviticus 19:1–2

# GOD REVEALS HIS NAME IN SCRIPTURE
## LEVITICUS 19:1–4, 9–18; ISAIAH 12:6

*Open your personal Bible translation and read the same passage. Make a mark where you read the word* **HOLY**, *the phrase* **I AM YAHWEH YOUR ELOHIM**, *or* **QEDOSH YISRAEl**.

**Yahweh** spoke to Moses, [2] "Tell the whole congregation of Israel: Be holy because I, **Yahweh** your **Elohim**, am holy.

[3] "Respect your mother and father. Observe my days of worship. I am **Yahweh** your **Elohim**.

[4] "Don't turn to worthless gods or cast metal idols. Never make any gods for yourselves. I am **Yahweh** your **Elohim**.

[9] "When you harvest the grain in your land, don't harvest the grain in the corners of your fields or gather what is left after you're finished. [10] Don't harvest your vineyard a second time or pick up fallen grapes. Leave them for poor people and foreigners. I am **Yahweh** your **Elohim**.

[11] "Never steal, lie, or deceive your neighbor.

[12] "Never swear by my name in order to deceive anyone. This dishonors the name of your **Elohim**. I am **Yahweh**.

[13] "Never oppress or rob your neighbor. Never keep the pay you owe a hired worker overnight. [14] Never curse deaf people or put anything in the way of blind people to make them stumble. Instead, fear your **Elohim**. I am **Yahweh**.

[15] "Don't be corrupt when administering justice. Never give special favors to poor people, and never show preference to important people. Judge your neighbor fairly. [16] Never gossip. Never endanger your neighbor's life. I am **Yahweh**.

[17] "Never hate another Israelite. Be sure to correct your neighbor so that you will not be guilty of sinning along with him. [18] Never get revenge. Never hold a grudge against any of your people. Instead, love your neighbor as you love yourself. I am **Yahweh**.

[6] "Shout loudly, and sing with joy, people of Zion! **Qedosh Yisrael** is great. He is among you."

## UNDERSTANDING THE NAME

*Qedosh* is Hebrew for "Holy One," a title for God that appears most frequently in the book of Isaiah, though it also appears in some of the other prophets (notably Hosea, Jeremiah, Ezekiel, and Habakkuk) and in Psalms and Job. It emphasizes God's otherness, separateness, and mystery. The term most frequently used for "holy" in the New Testament is *hagios*.

To understand the title "Holy One of Israel," Qedosh Yisrael (ke-DOSH yis-ra-AIL), we need first to understand that holiness is grounded in God's nature. It refers not to one of his attributes but to the totality of his perfection. In his holiness, God exists above and apart from the world he has made.

Things, times, places, people, and other created beings became holy by virtue of their connection to God. Thus, the people of Israel became holy because God had chosen them. Their holiness was to be expressed and maintained through ritual practices and adherence to moral laws, which set them apart for the service of God.

It is important to realize that God's holiness involves not just separation from sin but his absolute hostility toward it. Christ ultimately bridged the chasm between God and sinful human beings by making himself the perfect offering for our sins. Believers are called to be holy as he is holy and are enabled to imitate Christ by the grace of the Holy Spirit.

## CONNECTING TO THE NAME

1. In Leviticus 19, God links his commandments to his name. Why do you think he keeps reminding the people that he is "the Lord your God"?

2. If this were the only passage of Scripture you had ever read, what would it lead you to believe about God's character?

3. Notice that all the commands involve relationships. What kinds of relationships are high-lighted in this passage?

4. Read through these commandments prayerfully, asking the Holy Spirit to show you where you need to make changes in order to live according to God's guidelines for holiness.

5. What relationships in your life need attention, repentance, or forgiveness?

6. How can you pursue being generous, loving, honest, truthful, and just toward those in your sphere of influence? Think of some specific examples.

7. What would your life look like were you to live in the constant awareness that *Qedosh Yisrael* is great, that he is among you?

## PRAYING A PASSAGE WITH GOD'S NAME

Focus on the name **Qedosh Yisrael**, Holy One of Israel, as you read Isaiah 30:15.

This is what *Adonay Yahweh*, **Qedosh Yisrael** says:

> "You can be saved by returning to me. You can have rest.
> You can be strong by being quiet and by trusting me."

Thank God that we can be strong by resting in him rather than by giving in to our fears.

## PRAYING THE NAME **QEDOSH YISRAEL** FOR MYSELF

Look up and read: Isaiah 43:3

Consider the price God paid to ransom your soul from the power of evil. Praise him for the freedom that comes from living in his presence.

_____

_____

_____

_____

# PROMISES FROM **QEDOSH YISRAEL**

> [19] Humble people again will find joy in **Yahweh**.
> The poorest of people will find joy in **Qedosh Yisrael**.
> —Isaiah 29:19

[14] With one sacrifice he accomplished the work of setting them apart for God forever.

[15] The Holy Spirit tells us the same thing: [16] "This is the promise that I will make to them after those days, says the Lord: 'I will put my teachings in their hearts and write them in their minds.'"

—Hebrews 10:14–16

## FOR DEEPER STUDY

_Read the following passages, considering the name_ **QEDOSH YISRAEL** _and how its meaning relates to the context of the passage._

Psalm 71:21–23      Isaiah 1:4; 5:24; 6:1–7; 10:20; 30:15      Jeremiah 31:33

Hosea 11:1–9      Luke 1:35–36      1 Corinthians 5:9–13      1 Peter 1:14–16

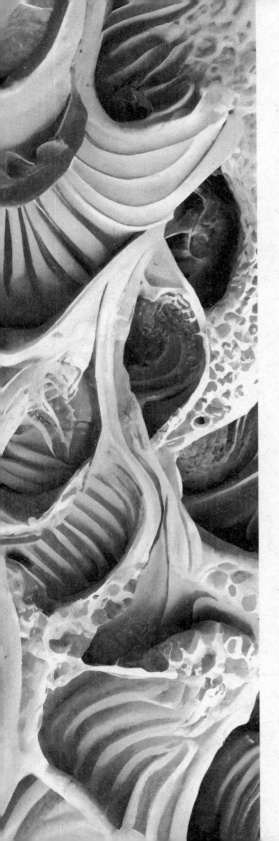

# THE LORD IS PEACE

## יהוה שָׁלוֹם
## YAHWEH SHALOM

Shalom is a Hebrew word, so much richer in its range of meanings than the English word "peace," which usually refers to the absence of outward conflict or to a state of inner calm. The concept of shalom includes these ideas but goes beyond them, meaning "wholeness," "completeness," "perfection," "safety," or "wellness." Shalom comes from living in harmony with God. The fruit of that harmony is harmony with others, prosperity, health, satisfaction, soundness, wholeness, and well-being. When you pray to Yahweh Shalom, you are praying to the source of all peace. No wonder his Son is called the Prince of Peace.

## KEY SCRIPTURE

So Gideon built an altar there to **Yahweh**. He called it **Yahweh Shalom**.

—Judges 6:24

# GOD REVEALS HIS NAME IN SCRIPTURE
## JUDGES 6:19–24

*Open your personal Bible translation and read the same passage. Make a note where you read* **YAHWEH SHALOM**.

¹⁹ Then Gideon went into his house and prepared a young goat and unleavened bread made with 18 quarts of flour. He put the meat in a basket and the broth in a pot. Then he went out and presented them to the Messenger of the LORD under the oak tree.

²⁰ The Messenger of **Yahweh** told him, "Take the meat and the unleavened bread, put them on this rock, and pour the broth over them." Gideon did so. ²¹ Then the Messenger of **Yahweh** touched the meat and the bread with the tip of the staff that was in his hand.

Fire flared up from the rock and burned the meat and the bread. Then the Messenger of **Yahweh** disappeared. ²² That's when Gideon realized that this had been the Messenger of **Yahweh**. So he said, "**Adonay Yahweh**! I have seen the Messenger of **Yahweh** face to face."

²³ **Yahweh** said to him, "Calm down! Don't be afraid. You will not die." ²⁴ So Gideon built an altar there to **Yahweh**. He called it **Yahweh Shalom**. To this day it is still in Ophrah, which belongs to Abiezer's family.

## UNDERSTANDING THE NAME

**Yahweh Shalom** (yah-WEH sha-LOME) is a title rather than a name of God. Shalom is a common term for greeting or farewell in modern Israel. When you say shalom, you are not simply saying "Hello," or "Have a Good Day." In its deepest meaning, it expresses the hope that the person you are greeting may be well in every sense of the word—fulfilled, satisfied, prosperous, healthy, and in harmony with themselves, others, and God. Shalom is a covenant word, an expression of God's faithful relationship with his people.

# CONNECTING TO THE NAME

1. The passage begins by revealing God as the disrupter of peace since he's the one who's handed the Israelites over to the Midianites. What does this reveal about the way God deals with his people's unfaithfulness and about the nature of true peace?

2. Think about a time in your life when you felt anything but peaceful. What caused your difficulties and how did you respond to them?

3. Why do you think the angel called Gideon a "mighty warrior"? Why did Gideon believe he was ill-equipped to be a leader and a warrior?

4. What comes to mind when you hear the term peace?

5. What might be stealing your peace? Do you have habits of worry and anxiety? Have you become too busy to seek *Yahweh Shalom*? Have you made compromises that have eroded your faith? Do you rely on news media to shape your perspective, distorting the deeper truths of your faith? Are you more connected to the culture than to Yahweh Shalom?

## PRAYING A PASSAGE WITH GOD'S NAME

Focus on the name **Yahweh Shalom**, the Lord of Peace, as you read Philippians 4:6–7. Thank God for making Jesus the source of our peace. Ask him to fill you with his Spirit, because to be filled with his Spirit is to be filled with peace.

> [6] Never worry about anything. But in every situation let God know what you need in prayers and requests while giving thanks. [7] Then God's peace, which goes beyond anything we can imagine, will guard your thoughts and emotions through Christ **Yeshua**.

### *PRAYING THE NAME* **YAHWEH SHALOM** *FOR MYSELF*

Look up and read: Psalm 122:6–8

"Peace be with you." Christ said it to his disciples and he says it to us. Is there anyone in your life to whom it would be difficult for you to say these words? Write a brief prayer for that person, asking that they would see Yahweh Shalom and feel his peace today.

_____

_____

_____

_____

## PROMISES FROM **YAHWEH SHALOM**

> [3] With perfect peace you will protect those whose minds cannot be changed, because they trust you.
> —Isaiah 26:3

## FOR DEEPER STUDY

*Read the following passages, considering what you've learned about* **YAHWEH SHALOM** *and how its meaning relates to the context of the passage.*

Numbers 6:22–27

Proverbs 3:13, 17

Isaiah 66:10–12

Jeremiah 29:11–14

Philippians 4:6–7

Colossians 3:12–17

# THE LORD OF HOSTS

## יהוה צְבָאוֹת
## YAHWEH TSEBAOTH

The Lord of Hosts is a title that emphasizes God's rule over every other power in the material and spiritual universe. When Scripture speaks of "the host of heaven," it is usually speaking of celestial bodies, though the phrase can also refer to angelic beings. The word "host" can also refer to human beings and to nature itself. When you pray to Yahweh Tsebaoth, you are praying to a God so magnificent that all creation serves his purposes.

## KEY SCRIPTURE

David told the Philistine, "You come to me with sword and spear and javelin, but I come to you in the name of the *Yahweh Tsebaoth*, the *Elohim* of the army of Israel, whom you have insulted. Today *Yahweh* will hand you over to me. I will strike you down and cut off your head. And this day I will give the dead bodies of the Philistine army to the birds and the wild animals. The whole world will know that Israel has an *Elohim*.

—1 Samuel 17:45–46

# GOD REVEALS HIS NAME IN SCRIPTURE
## 1 SAMUEL 17:38–47

*Open your personal Bible translation and read the same passage. Make note where you read* **YAHWEH TSEBAOTH**.

³⁸ Saul put his battle tunic on David; he put a bronze helmet on David's head and dressed him in armor. ³⁹ David fastened Saul's sword over his clothes and tried to walk, but he had never practiced doing this. "I can't walk in these things," David told Saul. "I've never had any practice doing this." So David took all those things off.

⁴⁰ He took his stick with him, picked out five smooth stones from the riverbed, and put them in his shepherd's bag. With a sling in his hand, he approached the Philistine. ⁴¹ The Philistine, preceded by the man carrying his shield, was coming closer and closer to David. ⁴² When the Philistine got a good look at David, he despised him. After all, David was a young man with a healthy complexion and good looks.

⁴³ The Philistine asked David, "Am I a dog that you come to attack me with sticks?" So the Philistine called on his gods to curse David. ⁴⁴ "Come on," the Philistine told David, "and I'll give your body to the birds."

⁴⁵ David told the Philistine, "You come to me with sword and spear and javelin, but I come to you in the name of the *Yahweh Tsebaoth*, the *Elohim* of the army of Israel, whom you have insulted. ⁴⁶ Today *Yahweh* will hand you over to me. I will strike you down and cut off your head. And this day I will give the dead bodies of the Philistine army to the birds and the wild animals. The whole world will know that Israel has an *Elohim*. ⁴⁷ Then everyone gathered here will know that *Yahweh* can save without sword or spear, because *Yahweh* determines every battle's outcome. He will hand all of you over to us."

## UNDERSTANDING THE NAME

**Yahweh Tsebaoth** (yah-WEH tse-ba-OATH) is a title of great power. It occurs more than 240 times in the Hebrew Scriptures, reminding us that all of creation, even in its fallen condition, is under God's rule and reign. At times Scripture speaks of the Lord of Hosts leading a great army. Cherubim and seraphim; sun and moon; stars and sky; rivers and mountains; hail and snow; men and women; animals, wild and tame—all these worship the Lord and are at times called to fight on his behalf. The NIV translates this title as "Lord Almighty."

## CONNECTING TO THE NAME

1. Why do you think the story emphasizes David's inability to do battle in the king's armor?

2. "I can't walk in these things, "David told Saul. "I've never had any practice doing this." David's statement seems to imply that he has walked a different way. What may David have practiced that led to his surprising victory?

3. Contrast David's attitude toward the battle with Goliath's.

4. Remember times in your own life when you felt embattled. How did you deal with your struggles?

5. How might your struggles change if you could trust *Yahweh Tsebaoth* the way David did? What if your heart could echo the truth that God "determines every battle's outcome?" What one thing could you do today that would help you face future battles with greater faith?

## PRAYING A PASSAGE WITH GOD'S NAME

Thank God that even when the nations are in turmoil and everything is shaking around us, he is with us and will prevail. Focus on the name Yahweh Tsebaoth, the Lord of Hosts, as you read Psalm 46:6–9.

> [6] Nations are in turmoil, and kingdoms topple.
>  The earth melts at the sound of God's voice.
>
> [7] **Yahweh Tsebaoth** is with us.
>  The **Elohim** of Jacob is our stronghold. *Selah*
>
> [8] Come, see the works of **Yahweh**,
>  the devastation he has brought to the earth.
>   [9] He puts an end to wars all over the earth.
>   He breaks an archer's bow.
>   He cuts spears in two.
>   He burns chariots.

## PRAYING THE NAME **YAHWEH TSEBAOTH** *FOR MYSELF*

Look up and read: Isaiah 9:6–7

God's plan of salvation included great humility, restrain, and seeming weakness on his part. Do you associate humility with victory? Reflect on Yahweh Tsebaoth's plan to save us, and ask him to show you how he can use weakness as strength.

# PROMISES FROM **YAHWEH TSEBAOTH**

O **Yahweh Tsebaoth**, blessed is the person who trusts you.
—Psalm 84:12

Tell the people, 'This is what **Yahweh Tsebaoth** says: Return to me, declares **Yahweh Tsebaoth**, and I will return to you, says **Yahweh Tsebaoth**.'

—Zechariah 1:3

## FOR DEEPER STUDY

*Read the following passages, considering the name* **YAHWEH TSEBAOTH** *and how its meaning relates to the context of the passage.*

2 Kings 6:8–23

Psalms 46; 148

Isaiah 14:24–27

# THE LORD IS MY ROCK

## יהוה צוּרִי

## *YAHWEH TSURI*

What better word than "rock" to represent God's permanence, protection, and enduring faithfulness? When you pray to the Lord your Rock, you are praying to the God who can always be counted on. His purposes and plans remain firm throughout history. The New Testament identifies Jesus as the spiritual rock that accompanied the Israelites during their long journey through the desert. He is also the stone the builders rejected but that has become the cornerstone of God's church.

## KEY SCRIPTURE

Thank **Yahweh**, my **Tsur**,
>who trained my hands to fight
>>and my fingers to do battle
—Psalm 144:1

# GOD REVEALS HIS NAME IN SCRIPTURE
## PSALM 144:1–2, 7–10

*Open your personal Bible translation and read the same passage. Make note where you see* **YAHWEH** *and* **TSUR**.

Thank **Yahweh**, my **Tsur**,
>who trained my hands to fight
>>and my fingers to do battle,
my merciful one, my **Metsuda**,
>my stronghold, and my savior,
>my **Magen**, the one in whom I take refuge,
>>and the one who brings people under my authority.

Stretch out your hands from above.
>Snatch me, and rescue me from raging waters
>>and from foreigners' hands.
>>>Their mouths speak lies.
>>>Their right hands take false pledges.

O **Elohim**, I will sing a new song to you.
>I will sing a psalm to you on a ten-stringed harp.
You are the one who gives victory to kings.

## UNDERSTANDING THE NAME

Rocks provided shade, shelter, and safety in the wilderness and were used to construct altars, temples, houses, and city walls. Heaps of stones were also used to commemorate important events in Israel's history. God's commandments, given to Moses, were etched on stone so that all generations would learn his law. The word "rock" epitomizes his enduring faithfulness. The Hebrew noun *tsur* is often translated "rock" or "stone," while *petra* is the Greek word for rock. To worship **Yahweh Tsuri** (yah-WEH tsu-REE) is to echo Hannah's great prayer of praise: "There is no Rock like our God" (1 Samuel 2:2 NIV).

## CONNECTING TO THE NAME

1. David praised God for delivering him from his enemies. What kind of enemies do you face or have you faced in the past? How have you dealt with them?

2. David expressed his sense of vulnerability with vivid images. Describe a time in your life when you felt particularly vulnerable.

3. How has *Yahweh Tsuri* heard your cries for help?

4. David describes God as a rock, fortress, stronghold, and deliverer. What do these descriptions reveal to you about *Yahweh Tsuri*?

5. Knowing that God is your rescuer and deliverer, how might this affect your temptation to defend yourself or retaliate against those who are against you?

6. How would your life be different if you experienced more deeply the truth that God is your Rock?

## PRAYING A PASSAGE WITH GOD'S NAME

Praise God for being the rock in whom you can always take refuge. Focus on the meaning of the name **Yahweh Tsuri**, the Lord Is My Rock, as you read 2 Samuel 22:2–4.

> **Yahweh** is my rock and my **Metsuda** and my Savior,
> [3] my **Elohim**, my rock in whom I take refuge, my **Magen**,
>     the strength of my salvation, my stronghold,
>         my refuge, and my Savior who saved me from
>         violence.
> [4] **Yahweh** should be praised.
>     I called on him, and I was saved from my enemies

### PRAYING THE NAME **YAHWEH TSURI** FOR MYSELF

Look up and read: Psalm 125:1–2

God brings steadiness to the chaos of our daily lives. He wants to be intimately involved. Imagine yourself surrounded by *Yahweh Tsuri*.

Psalm 125:1–2

_____

_____

_____

_____

_____

## PROMISES FROM **YAHWEH TSURI**

With perfect peace you will protect those whose minds
        cannot be changed,
        because they trust you.
⁴ Trust *Yahweh* always,
        because *Yah*, *Yahweh* alone, is an everlasting rock.
        —Isaiah 26:3-4

### FOR DEEPER STUDY

*Read the following passages, considering the name* **YAHWEH TSURI** *and how its meaning relates to the context of the passage.*

Exodus 17:1–6              1 Samuel 2:2; 7:10–12              Psalm 62:1–2

1 Corinthians 10:1–5       1 Peter 2:4–8

# THE LORD IS MY SHEPHERD

## יהוה רֹעִי

### YAHWEH ROEH

For at least part of their history, the Hebrews were a nomadic people, wandering from place to place and seeking pasture for their herds of sheep, goats, and cattle. To sustain their livelihood, it was vital for shepherds to keep their animals from straying, to protect them from thieves and wild animals, and to provide them with plentiful pastures. In the ancient Near East and in Israel itself, "shepherd" eventually became a metaphor for kings. The Hebrew Scriptures speak of God as the Shepherd of his people and apply this image to religious leaders as well.

The New Testament presents Jesus as the Good Shepherd, who protects the lives of his sheep by forfeiting his own life. When you pray to the Lord your Shepherd, you are praying to the One who watches over you day and night, feeding you and leading you safely on the path of righteousness.

## KEY SCRIPTURE

> *Yahweh* is my *Roeh*.
>> I am never in need.
>>> He makes me lie down in green pastures.
>>> He leads me beside peaceful waters.
>>> He renews my soul.
>>> He guides me along the paths of righteousness
>>>> for the sake of his name.
>> —Psalm 23:1–3

# GOD REVEALS HIS NAME IN SCRIPTURE
## PSALM 23

*Open your personal Bible translation and read the same passage. Make a note where you see* **YAHWEH ROEH**.

> *Yahweh* is my *Roeh*.
>> I am never in need.
>>> He makes me lie down in green pastures.
>>> He leads me beside peaceful waters.
>>> He renews my soul.
>>> He guides me along the paths of righteousness
>>>> for the sake of his name.

Even though I walk through the dark valley of death,
   because you are with me, I fear no harm.
      Your rod and your staff give me courage.

You prepare a banquet for me while my enemies watch.
   You anoint my head with oil.
   My cup overflows.

Certainly, goodness and mercy will stay close to me all the
   days of my life,
      and I will remain in **Yahweh's** house for days without end.

## UNDERSTANDING THE NAME

Shepherding was one of the earliest human occupations. A family's wealth was measured by how many sheep, goats, cows, horses, camels, and/or asses a man owned. Abel, Abraham, Isaac, Jacob, Moses, and David were all shepherds. Before David fought Goliath, he told Saul: "Your servant has been keeping his father's sheep. When a lion or a bear came and carried off a sheep from the flock, I went after it, struck it and rescued the sheep from its mouth. When it turned on me, I seized it by its hair, struck it and killed it" (1 Samuel 17:34–35 NIV).

It was the shepherd's responsibility to count each animal in order to make sure none had gone astray. At night, sheep were kept in simple enclosures, in caves or within walls made from bushes. At times, the shepherd would sleep with his body lying across the gate to the enclosure in order to keep the sheep safe. Though Israel's religious leaders were also referred to as shepherds, they were often chided for their failure to watch over the flock of God. Both then and now **Yahweh Roeh** (yah-WEH row-EE) is the one true Shepherd of his people.

# CONNECTING TO THE NAME

1. Read the first three sentences of this familiar psalm slowly, then close your eyes. Imagine that you are the sheep. What do you see? What do you feel?

2. What does it mean to "restore my soul"? Describe a time when you felt in need of such a restoration.

3. Read the fourth sentence slowly. Imagine again that you are the sheep. What do you see? What do you feel?

4. How has *Yahweh Roeh's* rod and staff protected, guided, or corrected you? How have you found comfort in them?

5. Why do you think the psalmist introduces the imagery of a table?

6. How would your experience of daily life change if you really believed that goodness and kindness would "stay close to" you all the days of your life? In fact the phrase could reasonably read, "Certainly goodness and mercy will chase me all the days of my life."

## PRAYING A PASSAGE WITH GOD'S NAME

Ask Yahweh Roeh, the Lord My Shepherd, for everything you need as you read Psalm 80:1. Thank him for being your shepherd.

> [1] Open your ears, O **Roeh** of Israel,
>> the one who leads the descendants of Joseph like sheep,
>> the one who is enthroned over the angels

### PRAYING THE NAME **YAHWEH ROEH** FOR MYSELF

Look up and read: Isaiah 40:10–11

Take a moment to pray with this passage in Isaiah, which tells about the real tenderness of God, the shepherd. He longs to gather you in his arms. How would you feel, gathered into the arms of Yahweh Roeh? Let yourself imagine it.

_____

_____

_____

_____

## PROMISES FROM **YAHWEH ROEH**

[14] I will feed them in good pasture, and they will graze on the mountains of Israel. They will rest on the good land where they graze, and they will feed on the best pastures in the mountains of Israel. [15] I will take care of my sheep and lead them to rest, declares **Adonay Yahweh**.

—Ezekiel 34:14–15

[14] "I am the good shepherd. I know my sheep as the Father knows me.[a] My sheep know me as I know the Father. [15] So I give my life for my sheep. [16] I also have other sheep that are not from this pen. I must lead them. They, too, will respond to my voice. So they will be one flock with one shepherd.

> [17] The Father loves me because I give my life in order to take it back again. [18] No one takes my life from me. I give my life of my own free will. I have the authority to give my life, and I have the authority to take my life back again. This is what my Father ordered me to do."
>
> —John 10:14–18

## FOR DEEPER STUDY

*Read the following passages, considering the name* **YAHWEH ROEH** *and how its meaning relates to the context of the passage.*

Ezekiel 34

Psalm 28:9

Isaiah 53

# THE NAME

## הַשֵּׁם HASHEM

Shem is the Hebrew word for "name" (the "Ha" before it is the definite article, "the"). The Bible speaks of Solomon's temple in Jerusalem as the place where God's name would dwell—the place where his people could pray and be heard. Jesus himself prayed that the Father would glorify his name through him. He also promised to do whatever we ask in his name. Philippians 2:9–10 (NIV) affirms that God has exalted Jesus and given him "the name that is above every name."

## KEY SCRIPTURE

> Nevertheless, my **Yahweh Elohim**,
>    please pay attention to my
>    prayer for mercy.
> Listen to my cry for help as I pray to
>    you today.
> 29 Night and day may your eyes be on
>    this temple,
>    the place about which you said,
>       'My name will be there.'
> Listen to me as I pray toward this
>    place.
>
> —1 Kings 8:28–29

# GOD REVEALS HIS NAME IN SCRIPTURE
## LEVITICUS 24:16

*Open your personal Bible translation and read the same passage. Make note where God speaks about his name in response to Solomon.*

[16] But those who curse **Yahweh's** name must be put to death. The whole congregation must stone them to death. It makes no difference whether they are Israelites or foreigners. Whoever curses **Ha-shem** must die.

## UNDERSTANDING THE NAME

God's name is associated with his glory, power, holiness, protection, trust, and love. To call on his name is to call on his presence. To act in his name is to act with his authority. To fight in his name is to fight with his power. To pray to his name is to pray to him. In fact, the very first mention of prayer in the Bible appears in Genesis 4:26: "At that time people began to invoke the name of the Lord (NIV)." Though we are to exalt God's name and proclaim it to the nations, it is also possible to dishonor it, which is the same as dishonoring him. God's name is his reputation.

Though God's name is holy and powerful, it cannot be invoked as a magic formula. Rather, his name becomes powerful whenever it is uttered by men and women who are exercising their faith in God.

Jesus taught his own disciples to pray by saying, "Our Father which art in heaven, Hallowed be thy name . . ." (Matthew 6:9 KJV). In John's gospel, Jesus prays to his Father, saying, "I have manifested thy name to the men which thou gavest me" and "I made known to them thy name, and I will make it known" (John 17:6, 26 KJV).

When we pray to **Hashem** (ha-SHAME), we are praying to the holy God who dwells in our midst, hearing and answering our prayers.

# CONNECTING TO THE NAME

1. What does it mean to confess God's name? What is the connection between repentance and answered prayer?

2. Why do you think Solomon prayed that God would hear the prayers of foreigners when they prayed toward the temple?

3. How can Solomon's great prayer at the dedication of the temple in Jerusalem inform your prayers today?

4. What does God mean when he says he will put his "Name" in the temple?

5. You are the temple of the Holy Spirit (see 1 Corinthians 6:19). Because the Spirit of God dwells in you, you can call upon his name at any time and in every need. What needs would you like to bring to Hashem right now?

# PRAYING A PASSAGE WITH GOD'S NAME

Thank God that we can experience victory over everything that threatens our souls. Focus on Hashem, the Name, as you read Psalm 20:7–8, taking a few moments to boast of his power and faithfulness.

> [7] Some rely on chariots and others on horses
> but we will boast in the name of *Yahweh*, our *Elohim*.
> [8] They will sink to their knees and fall,
> but we will rise and stand firm.

## PRAYING THE NAME HASHEM FOR MYSELF

Look up and read: Exodus 20:7

Humble yourself before God, and ask him to show you if you have ever take his name in vain. Keep in mind that it is possible to take his name in vain without ever resorting to profanity through hypocritical behavior, perjury, or falsely representing God's words or character.

_____

_____

_____

_____

## PROMISES FROM **HASHEM**

Turn toward me, and have pity on me
> as you have pledged to do for those who love your name.
> —Psalm 119:132

Because you love me, I will rescue you.
> I will protect you because you know my name.
> [15] When you call to me, I will answer you.
> I will be with you when you are in trouble.
> I will save you and honor you.
> —Psalm 91:14–15

### FOR DEEPER STUDY

*Read the following passages, considering the name* **HASHEM** *and how its meaning relates to the context of the passage.*

Psalms 61:8; 115:1; 119:55; 124:8

Isaiah 50:10–11

Acts 4:12

Ephesians 4:17

# KING

## מֶלֶךְ

## *MELEK*

The Israelites believed that Yahweh was Melek, or King—not just over Israel but over every nation on earth. They understood that the temple in Jerusalem was the earthly symbol of God's heavenly throne, and they expected a coming Messiah who would one day save his people from their enemies, establishing his rule over the whole world.

The New Testament presents Jesus as the King of Kings (see week 33), whose perfect obedience ushered in the kingdom of heaven. For the last two thousand years, God's kingdom has continued to spread through every nation, tribe, people, and language, as men and women accept Christ's rule. When you pray to *Yahweh Melek*, you are praying to the God who watches over the whole earth and who will one day come in glory to usher in an eternal kingdom of peace and righteousness.

## KEY SCRIPTURE

> Lift your hands, you gates.
>> Be lifted you ancient doors,
>> so that the **Melek** of glory may come in.

—Psalm 24:7

# GOD REVEALS HIS NAME IN SCRIPTURE
## PSALM 24:7–10

*Open your personal Bible translation and read the same passage. Mark each use of the word* **KING***.*

> 7 Lift your heads, you gates.
>> Be lifted, you ancient doors,
>> so that the **Melek** of glory may come in.

> 8 Who is this **Melek** of glory?
>> **Yahweh**, strong and mighty!
>> **Yahweh**, heroic in battle!

> 9 Lift your heads, you gates.
>> Be lifted, you ancient doors,
>> so that the **Melek** of glory may come in.

> 10 Who, then, is this **Melek** of glory?
>> **Yahweh Tsebaoth** is the **Melek** of glory! **Selah**

## UNDERSTANDING THE NAME

Compared to surrounding nations, the Israelites were relatively late in adopting monarchy as a form of government. Instead, they thought of Yahweh as their **Malek**. Once the monarchy was established, it was understood that the king received his power from God and was therefore responsible for ruling according to God's laws. David, Israel's second king, represented the ideal of how a king should rule.

But most of the kings of Israel and Judah fell far short of the ideal, leading people away from God by forging ill-fated alliances with foreign powers and by sanctioning the worship of false gods. After years of living under the rule of these less-than-perfect kings, God's people longed for a **Malek**— a descendant of David who would sit on Israel's throne, subdue its enemies, and then rule over the entire earth. Given these expectations, it is hardly surprising that even Jesus' disciples thought he would establish an earthly kingdom.

## CONNECTING TO THE NAME

1. Psalm 72 may have been a coronation prayer for one of the Davidic kings. Though it doesn't directly refer to God as the King, it does reflect the values of our heavenly King. Describe these.

2. How would the world be different if today's rulers reflected the values expressed in Psalm 72?

3. This psalm can also be read as a messianic psalm. How did Jesus fulfill this prayer?

4. How have you experienced Jesus' rule in your own life? What difference has it made?

5. Take a moment to list a few people and places in which oppression and violence reign. Pray for God's kingdom to come and his will to be done in troubled lives and desperate circumstances.

6. Do you eagerly anticipate the coming reign of the King of kings? In what ways might you have become complacent, living as if this world is all there is?

## PRAYING A PASSAGE WITH GOD'S NAME

Praise God for reigning over the whole world and ask him to extend his reign over and through you. Focus on the name Melek, King, as you read Psalm 97:1–4.

> **Yahweh** rules as king.
>> Let the earth rejoice.
>> Let all the islands be joyful.
> ² Clouds and darkness surround him.
>> Righteousness and justice are the foundations
>>> of his throne.
> ³ Fire spreads ahead of him.
>> It burns his enemies who surround him.
> ⁴ His flashes of lightning light up the world.
>> The earth sees them and trembles.

## PRAYING THE NAME **MELEK** FOR MYSELF

Look up and read: Psalm 47:7–9

We live in a troubled world, and it is sometimes difficult to reconcile God's kingship with the difficulties and tragedies that can be seen across the globe. Think of the most troubled places you can imagine, including in your own life, and pray the words of the psalmist, *"Elohim* is the *Melek* of the whole earth. Make your best music for him!"

_____

_____

_____

_____

## PROMISES FROM **MELEK**

*Yahweh* will be *Melek* over all the earth. On that day *Yahweh* will be the only Lord and his name the only name.

—Zechariah 14:9

"Then the king will say to those on his right, 'Come, my Father has blessed you! Inherit the kingdom prepared for you from the creation of the world.'"

—Matthew 25:34

## FOR DEEPER STUDY

*Read the following passages, considering the name* **MELEK** *and how its meaning relates to the context of the passage.*

Psalms 84:3; 97          Jeremiah 10:7          Matthew 13:24–30, 43

Hebrews 4:16          Revelation 21:1–4; 22:1–5

# HUSBAND

## אִישׁ *ISH*

Ish is the Hebrew word for "husband" in Hosea 2:2, 16. The word ba'al in the Hebrew Scriptures can also be translated "husband" (as well as "lord," "owner," or "master"), though this term usually refers to the Canaanite fertility god Baal (ba'al does occur in Hosea 2:16, "master"). Remarkably, in Isaiah and Jeremiah, this word is also used to describe God as the husband of his people, Israel. Though we never pray to ba'al, we do pray to the God who is the ideal husband, the one who provides for and protects his people and who refuses to divorce us no matter how unfaithful we may be. In the New Testament Jesus is presented as the bridegroom and the church as his bride.

## KEY SCRIPTURE

"On that day she will call me her **Ish**,"
declares **Yahweh**.
"She will no longer call me her
master.

—Hosea 2:16

# GOD REVEALS HIS NAME IN SCRIPTURE
## HOSEA 1; 2:5–7, 16, 19–20; 3:1

*Open your personal Bible translation and read the same passage. Make note where God calls himself* **ISH**.

[2] When **Yahweh** first spoke to Hosea, **Yahweh** told him, "Marry a prostitute, and have children with that prostitute. The people in this land have acted like prostitutes and abandoned **Yahweh**."

> She said, 'I'll chase after my lovers.
>> They will give me food and water, wool and linen, olive oil
>>> and wine.'

> "That is why I will block her way with thornbushes and build a
>> wall so that she can't get through.
> She will run after her lovers, but she won't catch them.
>> She will search for them, but she won't find them.
> Then she will say, 'I'll go back to my first husband.
>> Things were better for me than they are now.'

"On that day she will call me her **Ish**," declares **Yahweh**. "She will no longer call me her master.

"Israel, I will make you my wife forever. I will be honest and faithful to you. I will show you my love and compassion.

[20] I will be true to you, my wife. Then you will know **Yahweh**."

Then **Yahweh** told me, "Love your wife again, even though she is loved by others and has committed adultery. Love her as I, **Yahweh**, love the Israelites, even though they have turned to other gods.

 אִישׁ

## UNDERSTANDING THE NAME

God's passionate love for Israel is reflected in the Hebrew word **Ish** (EESH), meaning "husband." When it is applied to God in the Hebrew Scriptures, it symbolizes the ideal relationship between God and Israel. God is the perfect husband—loving, forgiving, and faithful, providing for and protecting his people. This metaphor of monogamous marriage between God and his people is strengthened in the New Testament, which reveals Jesus as the loving, sacrificial bridegroom of the church. Our destiny, our greatest purpose as God's people, is to become his bride. (For Jesus as the Bridegroom and Husband, see week 45.)

## CONNECTING TO THE NAME

1. Why would God tell Hosea to marry a woman who would break his heart and make a fool of him?

2. Put yourself in Hosea's place and imagine what you would feel like if your spouse were a prostitute or a philanderer. Now think about how God feels when his people stray from him. How do you think God responds to unfaithfulness?

3. What kind of love is expressed in these verses?

4. What encouragement for your own life can you take from the story of Hosea and Gomer?

5.  What encouragement can you take for the church?

6.  Have you settled for a relationship that keeps God at arm's length? In what ways could you lower your guard and start responding to him, believing that he is your ideal husband?

# PRAYING A PASSAGE WITH GOD'S NAME

Praise God because he has revealed himself as a husband of unlimited compassion. Focus on the name Ish, Husband, as you read Isaiah 54:5–7.

> Your husband is your maker . . .
>
> "Yahweh has called you as if you were
>    a wife who was abandoned and in grief,
>    a wife who married young and was rejected," says your
>       ***Elohim***.
> "I abandoned you for one brief moment,
>    but I will bring you back with unlimited compassion.

### *PRAYING THE NAME* **ISH** *FOR MYSELF*

Look up and read: Hosea 2:16

Warnings against idol worship can be found throughout Scripture. It's easy to think of idols as foreign objects, and ones that could be easily recognized. But, just by looking at the history of the Israelites, it seems like idols have always been insidious in nature, ready to slip into our lives

WEEK 18 | 101

without our notice. Humble yourself before God, your Ish, and ask him to show you if there are any idols present in your life.

_____

_____

_____

_____

## PROMISES FROM **ISH**

"Israel, I will make you my wife forever.
I will be honest and faithful to you.
I will show you my love and compassion.
—Hosea 2:19

Then I saw the holy city, New Jerusalem, coming down from God out of heaven, dressed like a bride ready for her husband.

—Revelation 21:2

## FOR DEEPER STUDY

_Read the following passages, considering the name_ **ISH** _and how its meaning relates to the context of the passage._

Song of Songs 8:6–7

Isaiah 62:4–5

Jeremiah 3:14, 20

Ephesians 5:25–30

# LIVING GOD

## אֵל חַי
## EL CHAY

Unlike idols of wood and stone, made by human hands, the Living God is himself Maker of heaven and earth. He alone is the source of our life. We live because he lives. The prophet Jeremiah reminded God's people that "every goldsmith is shamed by his idols. His images are a fraud; they have no breath in them" (Jeremiah 10:14 NIV). This title sets Israel's God apart from the false gods of the surrounding nations.

### KEY SCRIPTURE

and prayed to **Yahweh**, "**Yahweh**, **Elohim** of Israel, you are enthroned over the angels. You alone are **Elohim** of all the kingdoms of the world. You made heaven and earth. Turn your ear toward me, **Yahweh**, and listen. Open your eyes, **Yahweh**, and see. Listen to the message that Sennacherib sent to defy **Elohim Chay**.

—2 Kings 19:15-16

# GOD REVEALS HIS NAME IN SCRIPTURE
## 2 KINGS 19:9–19, 35–37

*Open your personal Bible translation and read the same passage. Make note where* **EL CHAY** *or* **ELOHIM CHAY** *is used as God's name.*

Now, Sennacherib heard that King Tirhakah of Sudan was coming to fight him.

Sennacherib sent messengers to Hezekiah, saying, "Tell King Hezekiah of Judah, 'Don't let the god whom you trust deceive you by saying that Jerusalem will not be put under the control of the king of Assyria. ¹¹You heard what the kings of Assyria did to all countries, how they totally destroyed them. Will you be rescued? ¹²Did the gods of the nations which my ancestors destroyed rescue Gozan, Haran, Rezeph, and the people of Eden who were in Telassar? ¹³Where is the king of Hamath, the king of Arpad, and the king of the cities of Sepharvaim, Hena, and Ivvah?'"

Hezekiah took the letters from the messengers, read them, and went to **Yahweh's** temple. He spread them out in front of **Yahweh** and prayed to **Yahweh**, "**Yahweh**, **Elohim** of Israel, you are enthroned over the angels. You alone are **Elohim** of all the kingdoms of the world. You made heaven and earth. Turn your ear toward me, **Yahweh**, and listen. Open your eyes, **Yahweh**, and see. Listen to the message that Sennacherib sent to defy **Elohim Chay**. It is true, **Yahweh**, that the kings of Assyria have leveled nations. They have thrown the gods from these countries into fires because these gods aren't real gods. They're only wooden and stone statues made by human hands. So the Assyrians have destroyed them. Now, **Yahweh** our **Elohim**, rescue us from Assyria's control so that all the kingdoms on earth will know that you alone are **Yahweh Elohim**."

It happened that night. **Yahweh's** angel went out and killed 185,000 soldiers in the Assyrian camp. When the Judeans got up early in the morning, they saw all the corpses.

Then King Sennacherib of Assyria left. He went home to Nineveh and stayed there. ³⁷While he was worshiping in the temple of his god Nisroch, Adrammelech and Sharezer assassinated him and escaped to the land of Ararat. His son Esarhaddon succeeded him as king.

## UNDERSTANDING THE NAME

Scripture constantly warns against the worship of false gods. The first of the Ten Commandments is itself a proscription against idol worship. The title **El Chay** (EL CHAY), the living God, emphasizes God's role as Creator of all that is, in contrast with idols made of metal, wood, or stone, which are merely the creations of human hands. Jeremiah paints a vivid picture, saying, "The customs of the peoples are worthless; they cut a tree out of the forest, and a craftsman shapes it with his chisel. They adorn it with silver and gold; they fasten it with hammer and nails so it will not totter. Like a scarecrow in a melon patch, their idols cannot speak; they must be carried because they cannot walk. Do not fear them; they can do no harm nor can they do any good" (Jeremiah 10:3–5 NIV). Imagine praying to a deaf and dumb god! That's exactly the case when someone worships any other God than El Chay!

## CONNECTING TO THE NAME

1. Sennacherib ruled Assyria and Babylonia from 705–681 BC. He invaded Judah in 701 BC and threatened to attack Jerusalem when King Hezekiah refused to pay taxes. How does Hezekiah's prayer reflect his understanding of El Chay?

2. Though Hezekiah asked God to deliver his people from their enemies, his prayer primarily focused on God's honor. How can his prayer be a model for ours?

3. How can this story of Hezekiah's reliance on the Living God to defend his people be applied in the lives of God's people today? In your own life?

4. We too have enemies with which to contend, though often these enemies come from inside (like anger, addiction, depression) rather than outside. What difficulties besiege you or someone you love today?

5. What lies do you need to reject in order to trust in the Living God's power to deliver?

6. Like Hezekiah did, what truths about God can you proclaim over these circumstances?

## PRAYING A PASSAGE WITH GOD'S NAME

Praise the Living God for being present with you today, revealing his love and his power. Focus on the name El Chay, the Living God, as you read Joshua 3:9–10

> [9] So Joshua said to the people of Israel, "Come here, and listen to the words of **Yahweh** your **Elohim**." [10] Joshua continued, "This is how you will know that **El Chay** is among you and that he will certainly force the Canaanites, Hittites, Hivites, Perizzites, Girgashites, Amorites, and Jebusites out of your way.

## *PRAYING THE NAME* **EL CHAY** *FOR MYSELF*

Look up and read: Psalm 84:2

Set your heart on *El Chay* because he is not a God of the past. He is alive *and* working in the world around you. Tell him of your longing to know his present power and his love.

_____

_____

_____

_____

_____

## PROMISES FROM **EL CHAY**

[9] The Samaritan woman asked him, "How can a Jewish man like you ask a Samaritan woman like me for a drink of water?" (Jews, of course, don't associate with Samaritans.)

[10] *Yeshua* replied to her, "If you only knew what God's gift is and who is asking you for a drink, you would have asked him for a drink. He would have given you living water."

[11] The woman said to him, "Sir, you don't have anything to use to get water, and the well is deep. So where are you going to get this living water? [12] You're not more important than our ancestor Jacob, are you? He gave us this well. He and his sons and his animals drank water from it."

[13] *Yeshua* answered her, "Everyone who drinks this water will become thirsty again. [14] But those who drink the water that I will give them will never become thirsty again. In fact, the water I will give them will become in them a spring that gushes up to eternal life."

—John 4:9–14

Can God's temple contain false gods? Clearly, we are the temple of the Living God. As God said,

"I will live and walk among them.
I will be their God,
and they will be my people."

—2 Corinthians 6:16

## FOR DEEPER STUDY

*Read the following passages, considering the name* **EL CHAY** *and how its meaning relates to the context of the passage.*

Deuteronomy 5:26

Psalm 42

Jeremiah 10:7–16

Daniel 6:16–27

Hosea 1:10

Matthew 16:13–16

John 7:37–39

2 Corinthians 3:2–3; 6:16

Hebrews 12:18–24

# DWELLING PLACE, REFUGE, SHIELD, FORTRESS, STRONG TOWER

מָעוֹן, מַחְסֶה, מָגֵן, מְצוּדָה, מִגְדַּל־עֹז

## Maon, Machseh, Magen, Metsuda, Migdal-Oz

These descriptive names for God often appear in clusters in the psalms as well as in other portions of the Scripture. When you pray to God your Refuge, Shield, Fortress, Dwelling Place, and Strong Tower, you are invoking the God who has promised to watch over you and keep you safe.

## KEY SCRIPTURE

"Whoever lives under the shelter of **Elyon**
will remain in the shadow of **Shadday**.
I will say to **Yahweh**,
"You are my **Machseh** and my **Metsuda**, my **Elohim** in
whom I trust."
—Psalm 91:1–2

# GOD REVEALS HIS NAME IN SCRIPTURE
## PSALM 91:1–16

*Open your personal Bible translation and read the same passage. Make note where you see the Psalmist call God* **MACHSEH** *or* **METSUDA**.

Whoever lives under the shelter of **Elyon**
will remain in the shadow of **Shadday**.
I will say to **Yahweh**,
"You are my **Machseh** and my **Metsuda**, my **Elohim** in
whom I trust."

He is the one who will rescue you from hunters' traps
and from deadly plagues.
He will cover you with his feathers,
and under his wings you will find refuge.
His truth is your shield and armor.

You do not need to fear
terrors of the night,
arrows that fly during the day,
plagues that roam the dark,
epidemics that strike at noon.
They will not come near you,
even though a thousand may fall dead beside you
or ten thousand at your right side.

You only have to look with your eyes
    to see the punishment of wicked people.

You, O **Yahweh**, are my **Machseh**!

You have made **Elyon** your home.
No harm will come to you.
    No sickness will come near your house.
He will put his angels in charge of you
    to protect you in all your ways.
They will carry you in their hands
    so that you never hit your foot against a rock.
You will step on lions and cobras.
    You will trample young lions and snakes.

Because you love me, I will rescue you.
    I will protect you because you know my name.
When you call to me, I will answer you.
    I will be with you when you are in trouble.
    I will save you and honor you.
I will satisfy you with a long life.
    I will show you how I will save you.

מָעוֹן, מַחְסֶה, מָגֵן,
מְצוּדָה, מִגְדַּל־עֹז

## UNDERSTANDING THE NAME

The Hebrew Scriptures reveal a God who dwells with his people—first in a tent in the wilderness and then in the Jerusalem temple. The New Testament takes this idea of God's dwelling place on earth a giant step farther by revealing a God who wants to dwell not merely with his people but within his people. Occasionally, Scripture reverses this imagery in a wonderful way by picturing God himself as our Dwelling Place or **Maon** (ma-OHN).

# מָעוֹן, מַחְסֶה, מָגֵן, מְצוּדָה, מִגְדַּל־עֹז

Closely allied to this image of Dwelling Place is the idea of God as our Refuge or **Machseh** (mach-SEH). He is pictured as one to whom we can run for safety and security. The word "refuge" also appears in the Hebrew Scriptures in connection to Israel's "cities of refuge" (the Hebrew word in this instance is *miqlat*), where people could flee for safety if they had accidentally killed someone. These cities were strategically located so that anyone in Israel was within a day's journey of one. A shield or **Magen** (ma-GAIN) is another image of God's protecting care. Ancient shields were often made of layered cowhide and were used in situations of close combat as well as to protect soldiers from rocks hurled from city walls.

In biblical times, some cities were enclosed by walls, twenty-five feet high and fifteen to twenty-five feet thick. Farmers worked in the fields by day and then retreated within the city walls at night for protection. Large, fortified cities also contained strongholds or strong towers that provided additional defense should the city's outer walls be breached. Like the other terms already mentioned, God is compared to a fortress or **Metsuda** (me-tsu-DAH) and to a strong tower or **Migdal-Oz** (mig-dal OHZ).

## CONNECTING TO THE NAME

1. What is characteristic of the person who experiences God as his or her refuge?

2. What is the link between loving God and experiencing his faithfulness?

3. One of the more unusual metaphors for God in the Bible is that of an eagle or a great bird under whose wings the righteous can shelter. Compare this with Jesus' more domestic image of a mother hen who longs to gather her chicks under her wings (see Matthew 23:37). How would your life be different if you were able to take shelter under "the wings of God"?

4. What do you think it means to rest in God? How have you experienced this rest?

5. What dangers does the psalmist list in Psalm 91? What promises from God does he cite?

6. What are the things you fear most? How can you apply God's promises to your fears?

## PRAYING A PASSAGE WITH GOD'S NAME

Thank God for being your dwelling place, your refuge, your shield, fortress, and strong tower. Focus on the names Maon, Machseh, Magen, Metsuda, and Migdal-Oz as you read Psalm 59:16–17.

> [16] But I will sing about your strength.
>    In the morning I will joyfully sing about your mercy.
>       You have been my stronghold
>          and a place of safety in times of trouble.
>
> [17] O my strength, I will make music to praise you!
>    *Elohim* is my stronghold, my merciful *Elohim*!

### PRAYING THE NAMES **MAON**, **MACHSEH**, **MAGEN**, **METSUDA**, AND **MIGDAL-OZ** FOR MYSELF

Look up and read: Psalm 61:1–3; 71:3

Recall a time that God has delivered you from trouble or danger. The psalmist talks of his own weakening. When did you know that you were too weak to take on the trouble on your own? What did Migdal-Oz do for you?

_____

_____

_____

_____

Look up and read: Psalm 2:2–3

God is steadfast in all times. Are you ever tempted to think, like the many voices that surround you, that God is not going to deliver you? Write a prayer of complete confidence, like the psalmist's, in the ability of Metsuda to shelter you and deliver you.

_____

_____

_____

_____

# PROMISES FROM **MAON, MACHSEH, MAGEN, METSUDA,** AND **MIGDAL-OZ**

> **Yahweh** will roar from Zion,
>> and his voice will thunder from Jerusalem.
>>> The sky and the earth will shake.
> **Yahweh** will be a **Machseh** for his people.
>> He will be a stronghold for the people of Israel.
>
> —Joel 3:16
>
> **El's** way is perfect!
>> The promise of **Yahweh** has proven to be true.
>>> He is a **Magen** to all those who take refuge in him.
>
> —Psalm 18:30

## FOR DEEPER STUDY

*Read the following passages, considering the names* **MACHSEH, MAGEN, METSUDA,** *and* **MIGDAL-OZ** *and how their meanings relate to the context of the passage.*

**DWELLING PLACE**

Psalm 71:3

Ezekiel 37:27

**REFUGE**

Deuteronomy 33:27

Psalms 46:1; 62:5–8; 73:28

Proverbs 14:32

**SHIELD**

Genesis 15:1

Deuteronomy 33:29

Psalms 3:2–3; 5:12; 28:7; 33:20; 84:11

Proverbs 2:7

Ephesians 6:12–18

**FORTRESS**

2 Samuel 22:1–3

Psalms 18:2; 31:3; 144:2

**STRONG TOWER**

Psalms 59:16–17; 61:1–3

Proverbs 18:10

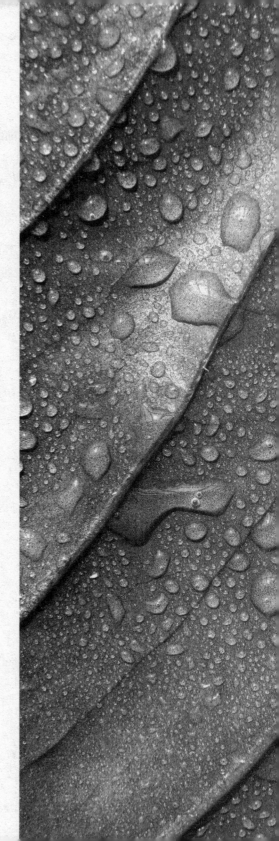

# JUDGE

## שֹׁפֵט

### *SHOPHET*

Justice is ultimately rooted not in a collection of laws or rules but in the very character and nature of God. As Judge of the whole earth, he is the only one competent to measure the motivations of our hearts. In the Hebrew Scriptures, the word "judge" is often parallel to the word "king." When we pray to God our Shophet (sho-PHAIT), we are praying to the one whose righteousness demands perfect justice but who has also provided a way for us to be acquitted of our guilt through the life, death, and resurrection of his Son.

## KEY SCRIPTURE

The decisions of judges will again
become fair,
and everyone whose motives are
decent will pursue justice

—Psalm 94:15

# GOD REVEALS HIS NAME IN SCRIPTURE
## PSALM 94:2–15

*Open your personal Bible translation and read the same passage. Make note where* **SHOPHET** *is used as God's name.*

Arise, O ***Shophet*** of the earth.
>    Give arrogant people what they deserve.
How long, O ***Yahweh***, will wicked people triumph?
>    How long?

They ramble.
>    They speak arrogantly.
>        All troublemakers brag about themselves.
They crush your people, O ***Yahweh***.
>    They make those who belong to you suffer.
>        They kill widows and foreigners, and they murder
>            orphans.
>            They say, "***Yah*** doesn't see it.
>                The ***Elohim*** of Jacob doesn't even pay
>                    attention to it."

Pay attention, you stupid people!
>    When will you become wise, you fools?
***Elohim*** created ears.
>    Do you think he can't hear?
>    He formed eyes.
>        Do you think he can't see?
He disciplines nations.
>    Do you think he can't punish?
>    He teaches people.
>        Do you think he doesn't know anything?
***Yahweh*** knows that people's thoughts are pointless.

O **Yah**, blessed is the person
>> whom you discipline and instruct from your teachings.
You give him peace and quiet from times of trouble
>> while a pit is dug to trap wicked people.

**Yahweh** will never desert his people
>> or abandon those who belong to him.
The decisions of judges will again become fair,
>> and everyone whose motives are decent will pursue
>>> justice.

## UNDERSTANDING THE NAME

The Hebrew verb **shapat** (sha-PHAT) can be translated in a variety of ways, including "judge," "govern," "vindicate," "decide," "defend," and "deliver." In the Hebrew Scriptures the word often combined the three primary functions of government—the executive, legislative, and judicial—that modern Western nations separate. That's why leaders like Gideon, Samson, and Deborah were called judges. When we read the Hebrew noun **shophet** (sho-PHAIT), "judge", in the Hebrew Bible, we need to remember that it often connotes the broader meaning of "ruler."

The prophets often chided Israel's rulers for failing to act justly, reserving their harshest words for those who ignored the rights of aliens, the poor, the fatherless, and the widow.

When the word "judge" is used in the New Testament, it tends to mirror the meaning of the word in Greek culture, emphasizing judicial functions rather than overall rule. The New Testament depicts Jesus as Judge of both the living and the dead.

# CONNECTING TO THE NAME

1. Who are the victims of injustice whom the psalmist names? How are such people still victimized in the world today?

2. What reason does the psalmist give for the brazenness of those who do evil? How does their perception of God still shape our own world?

3. Contrast the fool and the wise person as described by the psalmist.

4. How have you experienced Shophet's discipline in your life? What has been the fruit of it?

5. Why do you think justice is often something we have to wait for?

6. Why do you think that people sometimes object to the idea of God as a judge?

7. What would life be like if there were no such thing as justice? What would your life be like?

# PRAYING A PASSAGE WITH GOD'S NAME

Praise the Lord for his perfect justice and ask him to forgive you for times when you've been judgmental. Focus on the name **Shophet** (Judge), as you read Romans 2:1–4.

> No matter who you are, if you judge anyone, you have no excuse. When you judge another person, you condemn yourself, since you, the judge, do the same things. [2] We know that God's judgment is right when he condemns people for doing these things. [3] When you judge people for doing these things but then do them yourself, do you think you will escape God's judgment? [4] Do you have contempt for God, who is very kind to you, puts up with you, and deals patiently with you?

## PRAYING THE NAME **SHOPHET** FOR MYSELF

Look up and read: Psalm 96:10–13

We would do well to remember that God created the earth and has called everything in it "good," and that the right response to his creation is wonder, not judgment. What places and memories call up wonder in your spirit? Give jubilant thanks to **Shophet** for all the things that are good.

_____

_____

_____

_____

# PROMISES FROM **SHOPHET**

***Elohim*** is a fair ***Shophet***,
an ***El*** who is angered by injustice every day.
—Psalm 7:11

[34] "Then the king will say to those on his right, 'Come, my Father has blessed you! Inherit the kingdom prepared for you from the creation of the world. [35] I was hungry, and you gave me something to eat. I was thirsty, and you gave me something to drink. I was a stranger, and you took me into your home. [36] I needed clothes, and you gave me something to wear. I was sick, and you took care of me. I was in prison, and you visited me.' "

—Matthew 25:34-36

## FOR DEEPER STUDY

*Read the following passages, considering the name* **SHOPHET** *and how its meaning relates to the context of the passage.*

Psalms 72:1–19; 75:6–8; 96:10–13

Isaiah 11:1–9; 30:18

Matthew 7:1–5

John 5:24–27

Romans 2:1–4

# HOPE OF ISRAEL

## מִקְוֵה יִשְׂרָאֵל
## MIQWEH YISRAEL

Hope is the great stabilizer. It steadies us in times of fear and difficulty, not because we know that everything will turn out as we want, but because we know that God is trustworthy. Hope is what helps us stay on course regardless of circumstances. Biblical hope finds its roots in God and in his goodness, mercy, and power. We exercise our hope when we endure patiently. We nurture our hope when we read God's Word. Though we hope for earthly blessings, our greatest hope is aimed at the life to come, when God will not only wipe away our tears but invite us to share his joy forever. When you pray to *Miqweh Yisrael*, the Hope of Israel, you are praying to the one who saves all those who trust in him.

## KEY SCRIPTURE

Blessed is the person who trusts *Yahweh*.
　　*Yahweh* will be his confidence.
He will be like a tree that is planted by water.
　　It will send its roots down to a stream.
　　It will not be afraid in the heat of summer.
　　　　Its leaves will turn green.
　　It will not be anxious during droughts.
　　It will not stop producing fruit…

O *Yahweh*, the *Miqweh Yisrael*, all who abandon you will be put
　　to shame.
Those who turn away from you will be written in dust,
　　because they abandon *Yahweh*,
　　　　the fountain of life-giving water.

—Jeremiah 17:7–8, 13

# GOD REVEALS HIS NAME IN SCRIPTURE
## JEREMIAH 17:5–8, 13

*Open your personal Bible translation and read the same passage. Make note where* **MIQWEH YISRAEL** *is used as God's name.*

"This is what *Yahweh* says:

Cursed is the person who trusts humans,
　　who makes flesh and blood his strength
　　　　and whose heart turns away from *Yahweh*.
He will be like a bush in the wilderness.
　　He will not see when something good comes.
　　He will live in the dry places in the desert,
　　in a salty land where no one can live.
Blessed is the person who trusts *Yahweh*.
　　*Yahweh* will be his confidence.

He will be like a tree that is planted by water.
    It will send its roots down to a stream.
    It will not be afraid in the heat of summer.
      Its leaves will turn green.
    It will not be anxious during droughts.
      It will not stop producing fruit...

O ***Yahweh***, the ***Miqweh Yisrael***, all who abandon you will be put
to shame.
    Those who turn away from you will be written in dust,
      because they abandon ***Yahweh***,
        the fountain of life-giving water."

## UNDERSTANDING THE NAME

In the Hebrew Scriptures, hope is often connected to the expectation that God is a deliverer who will save those who trust in him. It urges us to wait confidently for him to act. In the New Testament hope is rooted firmly in Jesus—in his life, death, and resurrection as well as in his coming again in glory. We can also have hope for this life because the Holy Spirit indwells us, re-creating the image of Christ within us. Biblical hope is a new kind of strength, enabling us to be patient and enduring regardless of what we face. **Miqweh Yisrael** (MIK-weh yis-ra-AIL), the Hope of Israel—he is the God who saves his people.

## CONNECTING TO THE NAME

1. What does it mean to put your trust in people? Give some examples.

2. What does it mean to put your hope in the Lord? How have you been able to hope in *Miqweh Yisrael*?

3. Where are you tempted to place your hope other than in God?

4. Describe what you are hoping for in your life. How do your hopes connect with the promise implied by this title of God?

5. Think of a situation in your life for which you need renewed hope. What habits of thought undercut your hope and breed unbelief?

## PRAYING A PASSAGE WITH GOD'S NAME

Praise God for his righteousness and focus on the name Miqweh Yisrael, Hope of Israel, as you read Romans 15:12–13.

Again, Isaiah says,

"There will be a root from Jesse.
He will rise to rule the nations,
and he will give the nations hope."

May God, the source of hope, fill you with joy and peace through your faith in him. Then you will overflow with hope by the power of the Holy Spirit.

## PRAYING THE NAME **MIQWEH YISRAEL** FOR MYSELF

Look up and read: Lamentations 3:21–23

The Lord is our inexhaustible hope. Thank him because his compassion is new every morning.

_____

_____

_____

_____

## PROMISES FROM **MIQWEH YISRAEL**

Yet, the strength of those who wait with hope in *Yahweh*
will be renewed.
They will soar on wings like eagles.
They will run and won't become weary.
They will walk and won't grow tired.

—Isaiah 40:31

I know the plans that I have for you, declares *Yahweh*. They are plans for peace and not disaster, plans to give you a future filled with hope.

—Jeremiah 29:11

## FOR DEEPER STUDY

*Read the following passages, considering the name* **MIQWEH YISRAEL**
*and how its meaning relates to the context of the passage.*

Job 13:15     Psalms 33:16–19; 52:8–9; 119:81; 130:6–7     Isaiah 40:31

Jeremiah 14:8     Lamentations 3:21–23     John 16:20–22

Romans 8:28–38     Hebrews 6:19

# THE LORD OUR RIGH-TEOUSNESS

## יהוה צִדְקֵנוּ

### *YAHWEH TSIDQENU*

Righteousness isn't a popular word in our culture. Yet righteousness is essential to our happiness because it involves being in right relationship or right standing with God and conforming to his character, fulfilling our responsibilities toward him and others. But righteousness is impossible for us to achieve, no matter how much we long for it. It comes only as God's gift to us through faith in his Son. When we pray to the Lord Our Righteousness, we are praying to the one who has intervened on our behalf to restore us to his likeness and therefore to fellowship with himself.

## KEY SCRIPTURE

> In his lifetime, Judah will be saved,
> and Israel will live in safety.
> This is the name that he will be given:
> **Yahweh Tsidqenu**.
>
> —Jeremiah 23:6

# GOD REVEALS HIS NAME IN SCRIPTURE
## JEREMIAH 23:5–6; 31:33; ROMANS 3:21–25A

*Open your personal Bible translation and read the same passages. Make note where* **YAHWEH TSIDQENU** *is used as God's name.*

> "The days are coming," declares **Yahweh**,
> "when I will grow a righteous **Tsemach** for David.
> He will be a king who will rule wisely.
> He will do what is fair and right in the land.
> In his lifetime, Judah will be saved,
> and Israel will live in safety.
> This is the name that he will be given:
> **Yahweh Tsidqenu**."

"But this is the promise that I will make to Israel after those days," declares **Yahweh**: "I will put my teachings inside them, and I will write those teachings on their hearts. I will be their **Elohim**, and they will be my people."

Now, the way to receive God's approval has been made plain in a way other than the laws in the Scriptures. Moses' Teachings and the Prophets tell us this. Everyone who believes has God's approval through faith in **Yeshua** Christ.

There is no difference between people. Because all people have sinned, they have fallen short of God's glory. They receive God's approval freely by an act of his kindness through the price Christ **Yeshua** paid to set us free from sin. God showed that Christ is the throne of mercy where God's approval is given through faith in Christ's blood."

יהוה צִדְקֵנוּ

## UNDERSTANDING THE NAME

The Hebrew word **tsedeq** is usually translated as "righteousness" but can also be translated as "righteous," "honest," "right," "accurate," "justice," "truth," or "integrity." Righteousness primarily involves being in right standing with God. As such it concerns fulfilling the demands of relationship with both God and others. Though people were often called righteous in the Hebrew Scriptures if they observed the Law, Jesus and the writers of the New Testament stress that righteousness is not merely a matter of outward behavior but a matter of the heart—of thoughts, motives, and desires. The goal is not merely to do what God says but to become like him. In the words of Addison Leitch, righteousness "is primarily and basically a relationship, never an attainment. . . . Christian righteousness is a direction, a loyalty, a commitment, a hope—and only someday an arrival." The prophet Jeremiah predicted the coming of a King who would be called "The Lord Our Righteousness" (yah-WEH tsid-KAY-nu). Jesus fulfilled this prophecy by restoring our relationship with God through his life, death, and resurrection. Paul proclaims in his letter to the Romans, "But now a righteousness from God, apart from law, has been made known, to which the Law and the Prophets testify. This righteousness from God comes through faith in Jesus Christ to all who believe" (Romans 3:21–22).

## CONNECTING TO THE NAME

1. Jeremiah reveals that the coming King will be known as "The Lord Our Righteousness," as Yahweh Tsidqenu. What comes to mind when you hear the words "righteous" or "righteousness"?

2. What does it mean to have God's law written on your heart?

3. Why do you think God speaks of relationship—"I will be their *Elohim* and they will be my people"—right after he speaks of putting his teachings inside them?

4. How has Jesus' sacrifice affected your relationship with God?

5. In Romans 3:23 Paul writes, "There is no difference . . . for all have sinned (NIV)." How does this phrase affect the way you look at yourself in relationship to others?

## PRAYING A PASSAGE WITH GOD'S NAME

Thank God for sending his Son so that we could become right with him, ourselves, and others. Focus on the name Yahweh Tsidqenu, the Lord Our Righteousness, as you read 1 Peter 2:24–25.

> 24 Christ carried our sins in his body on the cross so that freed from our sins, we could live a life that has God's approval. His wounds have healed you. 25 You were like lost sheep. Now you have come back to the shepherd and bishop of your lives.

## PRAYING THE NAME **YAHWEH TSIDQENU** FOR MYSELF

Look up and read: Job 40:7–8

There are times when we, in our foolishness, think that we could do better than God. Humble yourself and repent before *Yahweh Tsidqenu* of the times when you wanted to critique his justice."

Job 40:7–8

_____

_____

_____

_____

## PROMISES FROM **YAHWEH TSIDQENU**

That which wicked people dread happens to them,
   but the Lᴏʀᴅ grants the desire of righteous people.
   —Proverbs 10:24

Blessings cover the head of a righteous person.
   —Proverbs 10:6

## FOR DEEPER STUDY

*Read the following passages, considering the name* **YAHWEH TSIDQENU** *and how its meaning relates to the context of the passage.*

Genesis 15      Job 40; 42      Psalm 23:2–3      Proverbs 10:6–25; 11:8

Ezekiel 36:26–28      Matthew 5:6      1 Timothy 6:6–12      1 Peter 2:24

# GOD MOST HIGH

## אֵל עֶלְיוֹן

### *EL ELYON*

When applied to God, the term Elyon, meaning "Highest" or "Exalted One," emphasizes that God is the highest in every realm of life. In the New Testament, Jesus is known as the Son of the Most High while the Holy Spirit is the power of the Most High. All who belong to Christ are revealed as sons and daughters of the Most High by imitating the Father in heaven. When you praise the Most High, you are worshiping the One whose power, mercy, and sovereignty cannot be matched.

## KEY SCRIPTURE

At the end of the seven time periods, I, Nebuchadnezzar, looked up to heaven, and my mind came back to me. I thanked the ***Illah-ah***, and I praised and honored the one who lives forever, because his power lasts forever and his kingdom lasts from one generation to the next.

—Daniel 4:34

# GOD REVEALS HIS NAME IN SCRIPTURE
### DANIEL 4:19, 24–34; PSALM 47:2

*Open your personal Bible translation and read the same passage. Make note where* **EL ELYON**, *or* **IL-ILLAH**, *is used as God's name.*

Then Daniel (who had been renamed Belteshazzar) was momentarily stunned. What he was thinking frightened him. I told him, "Belteshazzar, don't let the dream and its meaning frighten you."

Belteshazzar answered, "Sir, I wish that the dream were about those who hate you and its meaning were about your enemies.

"This is the meaning, Your Majesty. The *Illah-ah* has decided to apply it to you, Your Majesty. You will be forced away from people and live with the wild animals. You will eat grass like cattle. The dew from the sky will make you wet. And seven time periods will pass until you realize that the *Illah-ah* has power over human kingdoms and that he gives them to whomever he wishes. Since I said that the stump and the tree's roots were to be left, your kingdom will be restored to you as soon as you realize that heaven rules.

"That is why, Your Majesty, my best advice is that you stop sinning, and do what is right. Stop committing the same errors, and have pity on the poor. Maybe you can prolong your prosperity."

All this happened to King Nebuchadnezzar. Twelve months later, he was walking around the royal palace in Babylon. The king thought, "Look how great Babylon is! I built the royal palace by my own impressive power and for my glorious honor." Before the words came out of his mouth, a voice said from heaven, "King Nebuchadnezzar, listen to this: The kingdom has been taken from you. You will be forced away from people and live with the wild animals. You will eat grass like cattle. And seven time periods will pass until you realize that the *Illah-ah* has power over human kingdoms and that he gives them to whomever he wishes." Just then the prediction about Nebuchadnezzar came true. He was forced away from people and ate grass like cattle. Dew from the sky made his body wet until his hair grew as long as eagles' feathers and his nails grew as long as birds' claws.

At the end of the seven time periods, I, Nebuchadnezzar, looked up to heaven, and my mind came back to me. I thanked the *Illah-ah*, and I praised and honored the one who lives forever, because his power lasts forever and his kingdom lasts from one generation to the next.

We must fear *Yahweh*, *Elyon*.
He is the great *Melek* of the whole earth.

## UNDERSTANDING THE NAME

**Elyon**, the title given to the highest of the Canaanite gods, was appropriated by the Hebrews as a title for Yahweh. Emphasizing God's transcendence, the name **El Elyon** (EL el-YOHN) is first used in relation to Melchizedek, the king of Salem, who was also called "priest of God Most High" and who blessed Abraham in the name of "God Most High" (Genesis 14:18–20). The passage in Daniel regarding the interpretation of King Nebuchadnezzar's dream illustrates what happens when human beings forget who is highest in heaven and on earth. In Daniel, the Aramaic word **Illah-ah** is the equivalent of the Hebrew **El Elyon** and is translated as "God Most High."

## CONNECTING TO THE NAME

1. What does the king's dream and Daniel's interpretation indicate about the source of Nebuchadnezzar's greatness and prosperity?

2. Nebuchadnezzar may have been stricken by a rare form of insanity in which a human being believes he is a particular kind of animal. Why do you think his boasting led to this kind of punishment?

3. What does Nebuchadnezzar's story reveal about the link between sanity and humility?

4. El Elyon's blessings? Think, for example, about any tendency to take credit for your career, the gifts God has given you, or even well-behaved children.

5. If the good things of this life are clouding your vision of who El Elyon is, identify what or who is "most high" in your life. Is it God or something else—a relationship, a job, plans for your children, a dream for your future, an image of yourself?

6. What can you do to acknowledge God's greatness? Think of something specific you can do today.

7. When Nebuchadnezzar lifted his eyes to heaven, his sanity returned. When have you lifted your eyes to the Most High and had your perspective restored?

## PRAYING A PASSAGE WITH GOD'S NAME

Thank God that though he is Most High, he bends down to save us. Focus on the name El Elyon, God Most High, as you read Luke 6:35–36.

> [35] Rather, love your enemies, help them, and lend to them without expecting to get anything back. Then you will have a great reward. You will be the children of the Most High God. After all, he is kind to unthankful and evil people. [36] Be merciful as your Father is merciful.

PRAYING THE NAME **EL ELYON** FOR MYSELF

Look up and read: Psalm 97:9

*El Elyon* is exalted above all other gods. Humble yourself before him and ask him to protect you from the "other gods" that this world offers for your worship. Thank him for the gift of your faith, and ask him to strengthen you.

_____

_____

_____

_____

# PROMISES FROM **EL ELYON**

Whoever lives under the shelter of *Elyon*
will remain in the shadow of *Shadday*.

—Psalm 91:1

You, O *Yahweh*, are my *Machseh*!

You have made *Elyon* your home.
[10] No harm will come to you.
No sickness will come near your house.

—Psalm 91:9-10

## FOR DEEPER STUDY

*Read the following passages, considering the name* **EL ELYON** *and how its meaning relates to the context of the passage.*

Psalm 92:1–3                    Isaiah 55:8–9                    Acts 1:1–11

# THE LORD IS THERE

## יהוה שָׁמָּה
## YAHWEH SHAMMAH

Strictly speaking, **Yahweh Shammah** is a name for a city rather than a title of God. But it is so closely associated with God's presence and power that it has often been equated with a name for God, at least in popular parlance. The name in the New Testament that is most closely associated with it is *Immanuel*, "God with us," a name that was given to Jesus. **Yahweh Shammah** (yah-WEH SHAM-mah), "The Lord is there," reminds us that we were created both to enjoy and to manifest God's presence.

### KEY SCRIPTURE

From then on the city's name will be: **Yahweh Shammah**.

—Ezekiel 48:35

# GOD REVEALS HIS NAME IN SCRIPTURE
## EZEKIEL 37:21–28; 48:35

*Open your personal Bible translation and read the same passage. Make note where you see the name* **YAHWEH SHAMMAH**.

"Then tell them, 'This is what ***Adonay Yahweh*** says: I will take the Israelites out of the nations where they've gone. I will gather them from everywhere and bring them to their own land. I will form them into one nation in the land on the mountains of Israel. One king will rule all of them. They will no longer be two nations or be divided into two kingdoms. They will no longer dishonor themselves with their idols, with their detestable things, or with their rebellious acts. I will forgive them for all the times they turned away from me and sinned. I will cleanse them so that they will be my people, and I will be their ***Elohim***.

"'My servant David will be their king, and all of them will have one shepherd. They will live by my rules, and they will obey my laws. They will live in the land that I gave my servant Jacob, the land where their ancestors lived. They, their children, and their grandchildren will live in it permanently. My servant David will always be their prince. I will promise them peace. This promise will last forever. I will establish them, make them increase in number, and put my holy place among them permanently. My dwelling place will be with them. I will be their ***Elohim***, and they will be my people. Then the nations will know that I, ***Yahweh***, have set Israel apart as holy, because my holy place will be among them permanently.'"

"From then on the city's name will be: ***Yahweh Shammah***."

## UNDERSTANDING THE NAME

God doesn't entirely abandon sinful humanity after Adam and Eve are cast out of paradise in Genesis. Instead, God begins to reestablish his relationship with them. He starts by choosing a people for his own. Then he delivers his people from their slavery in Egypt, as Deuteronomy 4:37 says, "by his Presence and his great strength (NIV)." God dwells with his people first in the form of a pillar of cloud and fire, then in the movable tabernacle in the wilderness, and later in the Jerusalem temple.

But still God's people sin. Tragically, the prophet Ezekiel witnesses the glory of God departing from the temple because of their continued unfaithfulness. God is no longer there. Despite God's absence, the book of Ezekiel ends on a note of tremendous hope, predicting a time of restoration, when "the name of the city from that time on will be **Yahweh Shammah** (The Lord is there)."

## CONNECTING TO THE NAME

1. British preacher Charles Spurgeon once said that "whenever it can be said of an assembly, 'The Lord is there,' unity will be created and fostered. Show me a church that quarrels, a church that is split up into cliques, a church that is divided with personal ambitions, contrary doctrines, and opposing schemes, and I am sure that the Lord is not there." How have you experienced unity as a mark of God's presence?

2. What is the connection between keeping God's laws and living in his presence?

3. How do you experience God's presence in your life? Think back over the last week or the last month in particular. How has God been present with you in your work, your family life, your friendships, your difficulties?

4. Spend a few minutes imagining even one day of your life without God in it. Make a list of all the blessings of his presence that would be withdrawn.

# PRAYING A PASSAGE WITH GOD'S NAME

Thank God for being with you even when you don't know it. Focus on the name Yahweh Shammah, the Lord Is There, as you read Isaiah 43:2.

> When you go through the sea, I am with you.
>> When you go through rivers, they will not sweep you
>>> away.
>> When you walk through fire, you will not be burned,
>> and the flames will not harm you.

## PRAYING THE NAME **YAHWEH SHAMMAH** FOR MYSELF

Look up and read: Isaiah 63:9

Do you believe that Yahweh Shammah empathizes with you? That the things that trouble you also trouble him? Pour out your heart to him, imagining him as tenderhearted and concerned for you. Answer the question, "What's on your mind?"

_____

_____

_____

_____

# PROMISES FROM **YAHWEH SHAMMAH**

[19] That is why you are no longer foreigners and outsiders but citizens together with God's people and members of God's family. [20] You are built on the foundation of the apostles and prophets. Christ *Yeshua* himself is the cornerstone. [21] In him all the parts of the building fit together and grow into a holy temple in the Lord. [22] Through him you, also, are being built in the Spirit together with others into a place where God lives.

—Ephesians 2:19-22

[3] "The virgin will become pregnant and give birth to a son, and they will name him Immanuel," which means "God is with us."

—Matthew 1:23

## FOR DEEPER STUDY

*Read the following passages, considering the name* **YAHWEH SHEMMAH** *and how its meaning relates to the context of the passage.*

Exodus 33:12–17

2 Chronicles 6:41–42; 7:1–3

Psalms 132:13–16; 139

Zechariah 2:10–13

Matthew 1:23

1 Corinthians 3:16

Ephesians 2:19–22

# FATHER

## אָב
## αββα, πατήρ
## AB, ABBA, PATER

Though the Old Testament provides many rich names and titles for God, the New Testament reveals him most fully. Jesus, in fact, shocked and offended the religious leaders of his day by claiming that he had a Father/Son relationship with the God whose name they feared even to pronounce. Furthermore, by inviting his followers to call God "Father," he made this the primary name by which God is to be known to his followers. Because of Jesus, we can boldly pray the prayer he taught his disciples, "Our Father who art in heaven."

## KEY SCRIPTURE

So he went at once to his father. While he was still at a distance, his father saw him and felt sorry for him. He ran to his son, put his arms around him, and kissed him.

—Luke 15:20

# GOD REVEALS HIS NAME IN SCRIPTURE
### LUKE 15

*Open your personal Bible translation and read the same passage. Circle each instance you see the word* **FATHER** *used in the passage below.*

All the tax collectors and sinners came to listen to **Yeshua**. But the Pharisees and the experts in Moses' Teachings complained, "This man welcomes sinners and eats with them."

11 Then **Yeshua** said, "A man had two sons. 12 The younger son said to his father, 'Father, give me my share of the property.' So the father divided his property between his two sons. 13 "After a few days, the younger son gathered his possessions and left for a country far away from home. There he wasted everything he had on a wild lifestyle. 14 He had nothing left when a severe famine spread throughout that country. He had nothing to live on ... 17 "Finally, he came to his senses. He said, 'How many of my father's hired men have more food than they can eat, while I'm starving to death here? 18 I'll go at once to my father, and I'll say to him, "Father, I've sinned against heaven and you. 19 I don't deserve to be called your son anymore. Make me one of your hired men." '

20 "So he went at once to his father. While he was still at a distance, his father saw him and felt sorry for him. He ran to his son, put his arms around him, and kissed him. 21 Then his son said to him, 'Father, I've sinned against heaven and you. I don't deserve to be called your son anymore.'[a]

22 "The father said to his servants, 'Hurry! Bring out the best robe, and put it on him. Put a ring on his finger and sandals on his feet. 23 Bring the fattened calf, kill it, and let's celebrate with a feast. 24 My son was dead and has come back to life. He was lost but has been found.' Then they began to celebrate.

28 "Then the older son became angry and wouldn't go into the house. His father came out and begged him to come in... 31 "His father said to him, 'My child, you're always with me. Everything I have is yours.

# αββα, πατήρ

## UNDERSTANDING THE NAME

The Hebrew Scriptures normally depict God, not as the Father of individuals but as Father to his people, Israel. Pious Jews, aware of the gap between a holy God and sinful human beings, would never have dared address God as **Ab** (Hebrew) or **Abba**, the Aramaic word for "Daddy," which gradually came to mean "dear father." Jesus shocked many of his contemporaries by referring to God as his Father and by inviting his followers to call God "**Abba, Father.**" Rather than depicting God as a typical Middle Eastern patriarch who wielded considerable power within the family, he depicted him primarily as a tender and compassionate Father, who extends grace to both the sinner and the self-righteous.

The most frequent term for "father" in the New Testament was the Greek word **pater**. The first recorded words of Jesus, spoken to his earthly parents, are these: "Didn't you know I had to be in my Father's house?" (Luke 2:49 NIV). In John's gospel, Jesus calls God his Father 156 times. The expression "**Abba, Pater**" (AB-ba pa-TAIR) is found three times in the New Testament, all in prayer. It is the form Jesus used in his anguished cry in Gethsemane: "**Abba**, Father, everything is possible for you. Take this cup from me. Yet not what I will, but what you will" (Mark 14:36 NIV).

## CONNECTING TO THE NAME

1.  Who is Jesus speaking to when he tells the story of the wayward son? What might be a counterpart audience in our world?

2.  How have you experienced the kind of grace this father extended to his son?

3. Why do you think the wayward son fails to offer to become one of his father's hired servants, as he had planned?

4. How is grace offered to both the lawbreaker and the lawkeeper in this story?

5. With whom do you most identify in this story? Why?

6. Jesus does not tell us how the older son responded to his father's explanation. Why do you think the story is left open-ended?

7. What does this parable reveal about our heavenly Father, our *Abba*?

## PRAYING A PASSAGE WITH GOD'S NAME

Thank Jesus for leading you to the Father. Imagine yourself one of his flock and then focus on the name Abba, Father, as you read John 10:27–30.

> [27] My sheep respond to my voice, and I know who they are. They follow me, [28] and I give them eternal life. They will never be lost, and no one will tear them away from me. [29] My Father, who gave them to me, is greater than everyone else, and no one can tear them away from my Father. [30] The Father and I are one."

## PRAYING THE NAME **ABBA** FOR MYSELF

Look up and read: Deuteronomy 33:27

Imagine the Father's arms around you, destroying every enemy.

_____

_____

_____

_____

_____

# PROMISES FROM **ABBA**

The **_Elohim_** who is in his holy dwelling place
is the **_Ab_** of the fatherless and the defender of widows.
[6] **_Elohim_** places lonely people in families.
He leads prisoners out of prison into productive lives,
but rebellious people must live in an unproductive
land.

—Psalm 68:5–6

Don't be afraid, little flock. Your Father is pleased to give you the kingdom.
—Luke 12:32

## FOR DEEPER STUDY

_Read the following passages, considering the names **ABBA** and **PATER**
and how their meaning relates to the context of the passage._

Psalms 68:5–6; 103:13–14        Luke 12:32        2 Corinthians 1:3

Hosea 11:1–2        1 John 3:1–2        Matthew 5:43–48; 6:9–13, 28–32

# IMMANUEL

## עִמָּנוּ־אֵל
### IMMANU-EL

## ʼΕμμανουήλ
### EMMANOUEL

The name **Immanuel** appears twice in the Hebrew Scriptures and once in the New Testament. One of the most comforting of all the names and titles of Jesus, it is literally translated "with us is God" or, as Matthew's Gospel puts it, "God with us." When our sins made it impossible for us to come to him, God took the outrageous step of coming to us, of making himself susceptible to sorrow, familiar with temptation, and vulnerable to sin's disruptive power in order to cancel its claim. In Jesus we see how extreme God's love is. Remember this the next time you feel discouraged, abandoned, or too timid to undertake some new endeavor. For Jesus is still Immanuel—he is still "God with us."

## KEY SCRIPTURE

All this happened so that what the Lord had spoken through the prophet came true: "The virgin will become pregnant and give birth to a son, and they will name him **Immanuel**," which means "God is with us."

—Matthew 1:22–23

# GOD REVEALS HIS NAME IN SCRIPTURE
## MATTHEW 1:18—23

*Open your personal Bible translation and read the same passage. Make note when you see the name* **IMMANUEL**.

[18] The birth of **Yeshua** Christ took place in this way. His mother Mary had been promised to Joseph in marriage. But before they were married, Mary realized that she was pregnant by the Holy Spirit. [19] Her husband Joseph was an honorable man and did not want to disgrace her publicly. So he decided to break the marriage agreement with her secretly.

[20] Joseph had this in mind when an angel of the Lord appeared to him in a dream. The angel said to him, "Joseph, descendant of David, don't be afraid to take Mary as your wife. She is pregnant by the Holy Spirit. [21] She will give birth to a son, and you will name him **Yeshua** [He Saves], because he will save his people from their sins." [22] All this happened so that what the Lord had spoken through the prophet came true: [23] "The virgin will become pregnant and give birth to a son, and they will name him Immanuel," which means "God is with us."

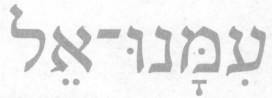

## UNDERSTANDING THE NAME

The name **Immanuel** (im-ma-nu-AIL) first appears in Isaiah 7:14 as part of a prophetic word that Isaiah spoke to King Ahaz of Judah (the southern kingdom) at a time when Aram and Israel (the northern kingdom) had formed a coalition against Assyria. The prophet Isaiah counseled Ahaz not to join in their uprising against Assyria; he urged Ahaz to trust in the Lord . Then the prophet invited Ahaz to ask the Lord for a sign to confirm the prophetic word, but the king refused.

In response to Ahaz's refusal to trust God, Isaiah proclaimed: "Therefore the Lord himself will give you a sign: The virgin will be with child and give birth to a son, and will call him **Immanuel**." Isaiah 7:14 NIV

Matthew's gospel recalls Isaiah's prophecy, applying it to the child who would soon be born to Mary (Matthew 1:22–23). The sign given hundreds of years earlier was meant for all God's people. In fact, the Bible is nothing if not the story of God's persistent desire to dwell with his people. In Jesus, God succeeded in a unique way, becoming a man in order to save the world not from the outside, but from the inside. **Immanuel**, God with us, to rescue, redeem, and restore our relationship with him.

Ἐμμανουήλ

## CONNECTING TO THE NAME

1. What does this title of Jesus reveal about his nature?

2. How have you experienced Immanuel— God being with you in your life thus far? See if you can recall a specific time in your life when God seemed especially near or think about all the small signs of his presence in your life.

3. When have you struggled to believe that God is living up to his name? That he truly is with you?

4. Matthew begins and ends his gospel (see Matthew 28:20) with the promise that God is with us. How would your life be different if you began and ended each day with the firm belief that God is with you?

5. Jesus said, "Never will I leave you; never will I forsake you" (see Hebrews 13:5). How should this truth affect your perspective, especially in difficult times?

6. Describe times in your life when you have not been with God. How might this have affected your experience of Immanuel?

## PRAYING A PASSAGE WITH GOD'S NAME

Thank God for his persistence in pursuing you. Ask him to increase your confidence in his desire to be with you. Focus on the meaning of the name Immanuel, God with us, as you read Psalm 139:7–10.

> Where can I go to get away from your **Ruach**?
> > Where can I run to get away from you?
> [8] If I go up to heaven, you are there.
> > If I make my bed in hell, you are there.
> [9] If I climb upward on the rays of the morning sun
> > or land on the most distant shore of the sea where the
> > > sun sets,
> [10] even there your hand would guide me
> > and your right hand would hold on to me.

## PRAYING THE NAME **IMMANUEL** FOR MYSELF

Look up and read: John 15:9–12

How can you remain one with Immanuel? In his conversation with his disciples just before his death, Jesus assures them that obedience allows them to live in his love. Ask God to lead you into deeper obedience.

_____

_____

_____

_____

## PROMISES FROM **IMMANUEL**

[11] But Moses said to *Elohim*, "Who am I that I should go to Pharaoh and bring the people of Israel out of Egypt?"

[12] *Elohim* answered, "I will be with you. And this will be the proof that I sent you: When you bring the people out of Egypt, all of you will worship *Elohim* on this mountain."

—Exodus 3:11-12

[20] Teach them to do everything I have commanded you.
"And remember that I am always with you until the end of time."

—Matthew 28:20

## FOR DEEPER STUDY

Read the following passages, considering the name **IMMANUEL** and how its meaning relates to the context of the passage.

Genesis 28:15    Exodus 3:11–12    Joshua 1:5–9    Isaiah 8:10

Matthew 28:20    John 14:15–21    1 Corinthians 3:16    Hebrews 13:5–6

# LIGHT OF THE WORLD

## τὸ φῶς τοῦ κόσμου
### TO PHOS TOU KOSMOU

According to Jewish tradition, one of the names for the Messiah is "Light." How fitting, then, that Jesus is called the "light of the world." John's gospel portrays Jesus as the light that vanquishes the darkness brought on by sin—a darkness that ends in death. Christ has opened the eyes of a sin-darkened world to the truth of the gospel. We who believe in him have moved from darkness to light, from death to life. When we pray to Jesus as the Light of the world, let us remember that we are calling on the one who was so determined to draw us into his light that he spent nine months in the darkness of his mother's womb in order to become one of us. Let us ask Jesus, our Light, to make us shine with his reflected glory.

## KEY SCRIPTURE

**Yeshua** spoke to the Pharisees again. He said, "I am the light of the world. Whoever follows me will have a life filled with light and will never live in the dark."

—John 8:12

# GOD REVEALS HIS NAME IN SCRIPTURE
## JOHN 1:3–9, JOHN 8:12

*Open your personal Bible translation and read the same passage. Make note where you read the word* **LIGHT**.

Everything came into existence through him. Not one thing that exists was made without him.

He was the source of life, and that life was the light for humanity.

The light shines in the dark, and the dark has never extinguished it.

God sent a man named John to be his messenger. John came to declare the truth about the light so that everyone would become believers through his message. John was not the light, but he came to declare the truth about the light.

The real light, which shines on everyone, was coming into the world.

**Yeshua** spoke to the Pharisees again. He said, "I am the light of the world. Whoever follows me will have a life filled with light and will never live in the dark."

# τὸ φῶς τοῦ κόσμου

## UNDERSTANDING THE NAME

The Hebrew Scriptures are full of images that link God with light—pillars of fire, burning lamps, consuming fire. Such images are often associated with God's nearness or his presence. John's gospel portrays Jesus as the embodiment of the divine light, a light so powerful that it cannot be overcome by the darkness of sin and death. Though Satan tries to disguise himself as an angel of light, he is light's opposite—the prince of darkness.

The phrase **"to phos tou kosmou"** (to FOHS tou KOS-mou)—the light of the world—appears three times in the New Testament (Matthew 5:14; John 8:12; 9:5). It is a distinctive phrase spoken only by Jesus, who uses it twice to refer to himself and once to refer to his disciples, who are to reflect his light through their good deeds.

Just as natural light is essential to life on earth, Christ's light is essential to unending life with God. Whoever believes in his light becomes like him, reflecting his brightness by walking in his light and obeying his commands.

## CONNECTING TO THE NAME

1. What do the terms "light" and "dark" mean to you?

2. Why do you think John's gospel uses images of light and darkness to describe Jesus and the world's response to him?

3. Have you ever lived through a time of darkness? Describe what it felt like.

4. Have you experienced Jesus as light? If so, how?

5. In Matthew 5:14 Jesus said, "You are the light of the world." In what ways have you been or can you be a "light-bearer" in places of darkness around you?

6. First John 1:5 says, "God is light; in him there is no darkness at all (NIV)." What does this mean to you?

# PRAYING A PASSAGE WITH GOD'S NAME

Ask God to shine his light into the deepest and most hidden places of your heart. Pray that he will bring his light and truth into these places. Focus on the name *To Phos Tou Kosmou*, the Light of the World, as you read 1 John 1:5–7.

> [5] This is the message we heard from Christ and are reporting to you: God is light, and there isn't any darkness in him. [6] If we say, "We have a relationship with God" and yet live in the dark, we're lying. We aren't being truthful.
>
> [7] But if we live in the light in the same way that God is in the light, we have a relationship with each other. And the blood of his Son **Yeshua** cleanses us from every sin.

## PRAYING THE NAME **LIGHT OF THE WORLD** FOR MYSELF

Look up and read: Ephesians 5:8–14

Ask the Lord to open your eyes and protect you from lies, especially the ones that you tell yourself. What lies have you believed but been able to renounce? What do you struggle to give completely over to the will of Jesus, to bring into the presences of Jesus and let him overcome?

_____

_____

_____

_____

_____

# PROMISES FROM THE "LIGHT OF THE WORLD"

The sun will no longer be your light during the day,
nor will the brightness of the moon give you light,
But **Yahweh** will be your everlasting light.
Your **Elohim** will be your glory.
[20] Your sun will no longer go down,
nor will your moon disappear.
**Yahweh** will be your everlasting light,
and your days of sadness will be over.

—Isaiah 60:19-20

[22] I did not see any temple in it, because the Lord God Almighty and the lamb are its temple. [23] The city doesn't need any sun or moon to give it light because the glory of God gave it light. The lamb was its lamp. [24] The nations will walk in its light, and the kings of the earth will bring their glory into it. [25] Its gates will be open all day. They will never close because there won't be any night there. [26] They will bring the glory and wealth of the nations into the holy city. [27] Nothing unclean, no one who does anything detestable, and no liars will ever enter it. Only those whose names are written in the lamb's Book of Life will enter it.

—Revelation 21:22-27

## FOR DEEPER STUDY

*Read the following passages, considering the name the* **LIGHT OF THE WORLD** *and how its meaning relates to the context of the passage.*

| | | |
|---|---|---|
| Exodus 34:29–35 | Psalm 27:1 | Isaiah 60:2 |
| Matthew 5:14–16 | Luke 2:29–32 | Acts 9:1–22 |
| Romans 13:12 | 2 Corinthians 4:3–6 | Ephesians 5:8–10 |
| Philippians 2:14–16 | 1 Peter 2:9–10 | 1 John 1:5–7 |
| Revelation 2:1–7 | | |

# CHILD

יֶלֶד

## YELED

παῖς

## PAIS

A child was always at the heart of the biblical covenant. Already in the garden of Eden God promised that Eve's offspring would crush the head of the serpent who beguiled her. Later God made a covenant with Abraham, promising that Sarah would bear him a child who would be the first of countless descendents. Then Isaiah spoke of a child who would be born of a virgin and be given the name "Wonderful Counselor, Mighty God, Everlasting Father, Prince of Peace." The New Testament tells of the fulfillment of that promise. Jesus presents children as the model for his followers to emulate. The only way to enter the kingdom is with the humility and trust of little children.

## KEY SCRIPTURE

So Joseph went from Nazareth, a city in Galilee, to a Judean city called Bethlehem. Joseph, a descendant of King David, went to Bethlehem because David had been born there. Joseph went there to register with Mary. She had been promised to him in marriage and was pregnant.

While they were in Bethlehem, the time came for Mary to have her child. She gave birth to her firstborn son. She wrapped him in strips of cloth and laid him in a manger because there wasn't any room for them in the inn.

—Luke 2:4–7

# GOD REVEALS HIS NAME IN SCRIPTURE
## LUKE 2:1–12

*Open your personal Bible translation and read the same passage. Make note where you see the word* **CHILD**.

At that time the Emperor Augustus ordered a census of the Roman Empire. This was the first census taken while Quirinius was governor of Syria. All the people went to register in the cities where their ancestors had lived.

So Joseph went from Nazareth, a city in Galilee, to a Judean city called Bethlehem. Joseph, a descendant of King David, went to Bethlehem because David had been born there. Joseph went there to register with Mary. She had been promised to him in marriage and was pregnant.

While they were in Bethlehem, the time came for Mary to have her child. She gave birth to her firstborn son. She wrapped him in strips of cloth and laid him in a manger because there wasn't any room for them in the inn.

Shepherds were in the fields near Bethlehem. They were taking turns watching their flock during the night. An angel from the Lord suddenly appeared to them. The glory of the Lord filled the area with light, and they were terrified. The angel said to them, "Don't be afraid! I have good news for you, a message that will fill everyone with joy. Today your Savior, Christ the Lord, was born in David's city. This is how you will recognize him: You will find an infant wrapped in strips of cloth and lying in a manger."

# παῖς יֶלֶד

## UNDERSTANDING THE NAME

Though the Israelites considered children a great blessing, children occupied the bottom rung of the social ladder. Entrusted with the solemn responsibility of teaching and disciplining them, parents were accorded nearly absolute authority. To be a child was to be powerless, dependent, subservient. Yet even little children and young infants could receive wisdom from God and their lips could praise him. The prophet Isaiah spoke of a child, or **yeled** (YEL-ed), who would one day be born of a virgin and sit on David's throne. Luke's gospel tells us that Mary, while she was yet betrothed, was expecting a child, or **pais** (PICE), and that she gave birth to him in Bethlehem.

## CONNECTING TO THE NAME

1. What images come to mind when you think of the child Jesus?

2. Why does Luke make a point of mentioning that Jesus was born in Bethlehem and that he was Mary's son?

3. Why do you think God allowed his Son to be born under the shadow of scandal and in such humble circumstances and to be placed in a manger?

4. The Savior of the world, heralded by angels, came as a helpless, dependent, vulnerable child. Why do you think God chose this means of bringing us our Savior?

5. If Christ made himself vulnerable in order to win the world, what implications does this have for the way you live as his follower?

6. Why might God's plan offend some people or seem like "foolishness"? What obstacles did this plan pose for many who encountered Jesus? For those who encounter him today?

7. What elements of the gospel still strike you as "foolish," things that are easier to read about than put into practice?

8. Jesus said to his disciples, "Unless you change and become like little children, you will never enter the kingdom of heaven. Therefore, whoever humbles himself like this child is greatest in the kingdom of heaven" (see Matthew 18:3–4). What does this admonition to become like a little child mean for your own life?

## PRAYING A PASSAGE WITH GOD'S NAME

Praise God who kept his centuries-long promise to send a child to save us. Focus on the name Yeled, Child, as you read Luke 1:39–45.

> [39] Soon afterward, Mary hurried to a city in the mountain region of Judah. [40] She entered Zechariah's home and greeted Elizabeth.
>
> [41] When Elizabeth heard the greeting, she felt the baby kick. Elizabeth was filled with the Holy Spirit. [42] She said in a loud voice, "You are the most blessed of all women, and blessed is the child that you will have. [43] I feel blessed that the mother of my Lord is visiting me. [44] As soon as I heard your greeting, I felt the baby jump for joy. [45] You are blessed for believing that the Lord would keep his promise to you."

## PRAYING THE NAME **CHILD** FOR MYSELF

Look up and read: Matthew 18:1–5

Jesus was the long-awaited Yeled, Child, who came for our sake. Ask him how you can be more childlike and trusting. Pray with these verses, and ask him to help you to believe in him in all circumstances.

## PROMISES FROM JESUS, THE **CHILD**

¹⁴ So **Yahweh Elohim** said to the snake, "Because you have done this,

> You are cursed more than all the wild or domestic animals.
> You will crawl on your belly.
> You will be the lowest of animals as long as you live.
> ¹⁵ I will make you and the woman hostile toward each other.
> I will make your descendants
>     and her descendant hostile toward each other.
> He will crush your head,
>     and you will bruise his heel."
>
> —Genesis 3:14-15

¹⁴ So **Adonay** himself will give you this sign: A virgin will become pregnant and give birth to a son, and she will name him Immanuel [God Is With Us].

—Isaiah 7:14

## FOR DEEPER STUDY

*Read the following passages, considering the name* **CHILD** *and how its meaning relates to the context of the passage.*

Isaiah 9:6–7          Luke 2:1–20; 9:48          1 Corinthians 1:18–31

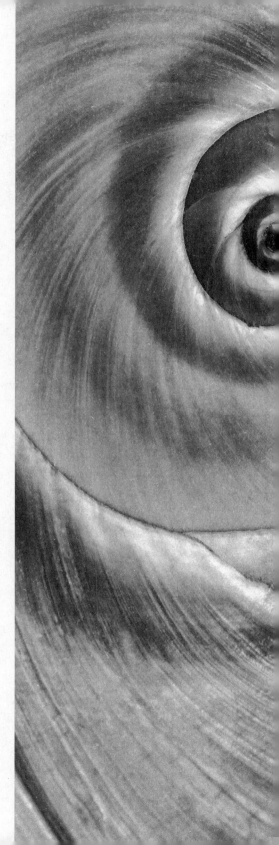

# BREAD OF LIFE

## ἄρτος ζωῆς
### ARTOS ZOES

Without bread no one in ancient Palestine would have survived for long. So it seems entirely reasonable for Jesus, in what has become known as the Lord's Prayer, to instruct his disciples to pray for their daily bread. Yet the Lord also challenged his followers not to work for food that spoils, announcing himself as the only food that would enable them to live forever.

In fact, Jesus was born in Bethlehem, which means "house of bread." After feeding five thousand people with only five loaves of bread and two fish, he shocked his listeners by declaring: "Unless you eat the flesh of the Son of Man and drink his blood, you have no life in you" (John 6:53 NIV). This week, as you seek to understand what it means that Jesus is the Bread of Life, ask him to show you exactly what it means to feed on him.

## KEY SCRIPTURE

"I am the bread of life. Your ancestors ate the manna in the desert and died. This is the bread that comes from heaven so that whoever eats it won't die. I am the living bread that came from heaven. Whoever eats this bread will live forever. The bread I will give to bring life to the world is my flesh."

—John 6:48–51

# GOD REVEALS HIS NAME IN SCRIPTURE
### JOHN 6:25–27, 48–58

*Open your personal Bible translation and read the same passage. Make note where you see the word* **BREAD** *or the phrase* **BREAD OF LIFE**.

When they found him on the other side of the sea, they asked him, "Rabbi, when did you get here?"

**Yeshua** replied to them, "I can guarantee this truth: You're not looking for me because you saw miracles. You are looking for me because you ate as much of those loaves as you wanted. Don't work for food that spoils. Instead, work for the food that lasts into eternal life. This is the food the Son of Man will give you. After all, the Father has placed his seal of approval on him."

"I am the bread of life. Your ancestors ate the manna in the desert and died. This is the bread that comes from heaven so that whoever eats it won't die. I am the living bread that came from heaven. Whoever eats this bread will live forever. The bread I will give to bring life to the world is my flesh."

The Jews began to quarrel with each other. They said, "How can this man give us his flesh to eat?"

Jesus told them, "I can guarantee this truth: If you don't eat the flesh of the Son of Man and drink his blood, you don't have the source of life in you. Those who eat my flesh and drink my blood have eternal life, and I will bring them back to life on the last day. My flesh is true food, and my blood is true drink. Those who eat my flesh and drink my blood live in me, and I live in them. The Father who has life sent me, and I live because of the Father. So those who feed on me will live because of me. This is the bread that came from heaven. It is not like the bread your ancestors ate. They eventually died. Those who eat this bread will live forever."

## UNDERSTANDING THE NAME

Bread was baked daily in the ancient world. Made from a variety of grains (barley for the poor and wheat for those with money), it was usually shaped into small round loaves that looked more like rolls or buns than the large loaves of bread we eat today.

Because bread was a primary staple, it was also used in various aspects of worship. Cereal offerings took the form of loaves or cakes, and bread was also used as a first fruit offering or as a peace offering. The **Bread of the Presence**, consisting of twelve loaves of unleavened bread, symbolized the covenant between God and his people. Displayed in the temple sanctuary next to the Most Holy Place, it served as a constant reminder to the priests and the people that it was God who sustained the twelve tribes of Israel in the desert. Psalm 78:24–25 (NIV) speaks of how God's people were fed in the wilderness:

> "He [God] rained down manna for the people to eat,
>    he gave them the grain of heaven.
> Human beings ate the bread of angels;
>    he sent them all the food they could eat."

Bread also played an important role in the Feast of Unleavened Bread. In fact, the bread that was consumed at the Last Supper, as well as the bread Jesus shared with the two travelers in Emmaus, was probably unleavened bread since both meals occurred during Passover Week.

In John's Gospel, Jesus called himself **Artos Zoes** (AR-tos zo-ASE), the **Bread of Life**.

# CONNECTING TO THE NAME

1. We live in an affluent, consumer-driven society in which "cheap bread" is sold on every corner. Give some examples of the food that fails to nourish.

2. Jesus knew that bread is one of life's necessities, yet he counseled his followers not to work for food that spoils. What are the implications for your life?

3. What do you hunger and thirst for that does not bring life to you?

4. Various Christian denominations have interpreted Jesus' words about eating his flesh and drinking his blood differently. How have these words impacted your own spiritual journey?

5. Discuss the various ways in which it is possible for you to "feed on Jesus, The Bread of Life."

# PRAYING A PASSAGE WITH GOD'S NAME

Praise Christ for being and providing the Bread of Life. Thank him for revealing himself to us as bread that is broken. Focus on the name Artos Zoes, the Bread of Life, as you read Luke 24:30–32.

> [30] While he was at the table with them, he took bread and blessed it. He broke the bread and gave it to them. [31] Then their eyes were opened, and they recognized him. But he vanished from their sight.
>
> [32] They said to each other, "Weren't we excited when he talked with us on the road and opened up the meaning of the Scriptures for us?"

## PRAYING THE NAME **THE BREAD OF LIFE** FOR MYSELF

Look up and read: John 6:53–58

Jesus is the source of life for his followers. Many in the crowd could not believe Jesus when he declared himself to be the bread of life, and many in the world today cannot believe it either. What messages do you hear from the world about the source of life? Write a prayer renouncing these false sources and telling Jesus he is Artos Zoes.

_____

_____

_____

_____

_____

## PROMISES FROM THE **BREAD OF LIFE**

[35] *Yeshua* told them, "I am the bread of life. Whoever comes to me will never become hungry, and whoever believes in me will never become thirsty.

—John 6:35

[48] "I am the bread of life. [49] Your ancestors ate the manna in the desert and died. [50] This is the bread that comes from heaven so that whoever eats it won't die. [51] I am the living bread that came from heaven. Whoever eats this bread will live forever. The bread I will give to bring life to the world is my flesh."

—John 6:48-51

### FOR DEEPER STUDY

*Read the following passages, considering the name* **THE BREAD OF LIFE** *and how its meaning relates to the context of the passage.*

Exodus 16:4–19

Isaiah 55:1–2

Luke 22:7–22; 24:13–35

Revelation 2:17

# PHYSICIAN

## ἰατρός
### IATROS

Jesus, the greatest of all physicians, performed more healings than any other kind of miracle. Nothing stumped him—not blindness, mental illness, lameness, deafness, or even death. Every ailment yielded to his undeniable power, and every healing served as evidence that his kingdom was breaking into our fallen world. When you pray for healing for yourself or others, remember that God never sends sickness, though he sometimes allows us to become sick. Indeed, Scripture sees sickness and death as by-products of sin. And it was to solve the sin problem that Jesus came into the world. When you pray for healing, remember that Jesus is always your ally, always wanting what is best for you and for those you care about.

## KEY SCRIPTURES

So he said to them, "You'll probably quote this proverb to me, 'Doctor, cure yourself!' and then say to me, 'Do all the things in your hometown that we've heard you've done in Capernaum.'"

—Luke 4:23

# GOD REVEALS HIS NAME IN SCRIPTURE
## LUKE 4:16–24

*Open your personal Bible translation and read the same passage. Make note where you see the word* **DOCTOR** *or phrases about healing.*

Then **Yeshua** came to Nazareth, where he had been brought up. As usual he went into the synagogue on the day of worship. He stood up to read the lesson. The attendant gave him the book of the prophet Isaiah. He opened it and found the place where it read:

> "The Spirit of the Lord is with me.
>     He has anointed me
>         to tell the Good News to the poor.
>     He has sent me
>         to announce forgiveness to the prisoners of sin
>             and the restoring of sight to the blind,
>         to forgive those who have been shattered by sin,
>     to announce the year of the Lord's favor."

**Yeshua** closed the book, gave it back to the attendant, and sat down. Everyone in the synagogue watched him closely. Then he said to them, "This passage came true today when you heard me read it."

All the people spoke well of him. They were amazed to hear the gracious words flowing from his lips. They said, "Isn't this Joseph's son?"

So he said to them, "You'll probably quote this proverb to me, 'Doctor, cure yourself!' and then say to me, 'Do all the things in your hometown that we've heard you've done in Capernaum.'" Then **Yeshua** added, "I can guarantee this truth: A prophet isn't accepted in his hometown.

ἰατρός

## UNDERSTANDING THE NAME

Though the Jews used physicians, they believed healing came ultimately from God. He was *Yahweh Rophe*, "the Lord Who Heals." What's more, their Divine Healer had given them a set of laws that included hygienic practices that contributed to their health and to their staying power as a people. Also, according to the Talmud, an authoritative collection of Jewish writings, every city had its own doctor who was licensed by city officials. The temple in Jerusalem also had its own physician, assigned to take care of the priests.

Jesus' healing miracles clearly reveal him as the greatest of all physicians. While he emphasized the importance of faith in the healing process, the Gospels do not support the teaching that a lack of healing always indicates a lack of faith. Scripture does not presume that every sickness is caused by individual sin. Rather, human beings become ill as the result of living in a fallen world.

It is interesting to note that the author of Luke's gospel, which recounts many of Jesus' healing miracles, was himself a physician (see Colossians 4:14).

## CONNECTING TO THE NAME

1. Why do you think Jesus responded to John the Baptist in the way he did in Matthew 11:2–5? What does this say about his purpose for coming into the world?

2. In Luke's gospel, in a rather roundabout way, Jesus refers to himself as a "physician." Yet his words indicate that his work as a physician would not always be well received. Why do you think this was so?

3. Do you think Jesus still heals people today? Why or why not?

4. Are there areas of your life, physical, emotional, or spiritual, that need the healing touch of the great Physician?

5. Sometimes we have difficulty believing in God's healing power. If you struggle with this, describe what hinders you from trusting him to heal.

6. Have you experienced God's healing power in your own life? If so, how?

## PRAYING A PASSAGE WITH GOD'S NAME

Praise God for his healing power and confess any sins that relate directly to your body, such as sexual sins, intemperance, gluttony, or sloth. Focus on the meaning of the name *Iatros*, "Physician," as you read Matthew 9:2–8.

> [2] Some people brought him a paralyzed man on a stretcher.
>
> When **Yeshua** saw their faith, he said to the man, "Cheer up, friend! Your sins are forgiven."
>
> [3] Then some of the experts in Moses' Teachings thought, "He's dishonoring God."
>
> [4] **Yeshua** knew what they were thinking. He asked them, "Why are you thinking evil things? [5] Is it easier to say, 'Your sins are forgiven,' or to say, 'Get up and walk'? [6] I want you to know that the Son of Man has authority on earth to forgive sins." Then he said to the paralyzed man, "Get up, pick up your stretcher, and go home."
>
> [7] So the man got up and went home. [8] When the crowd saw this, they were filled with awe and praised God for giving such authority to humans.

*PRAYING THE NAME* **PHYSICIAN** *FOR MYSELF*

Look up and read: Luke 8:43–46

The woman who touches Jesus' clothes in these verses had been suffering for a very long time. Are there any sorrows that you've carried for a number of years, sorrows that you would feel embarrassed to bring up? Humble yourself, and ask the Great Physician to heal you.

## PROMISES FROM JESUS, OUR **PHYSICIAN**

[13] I may shut the sky so that there is no rain,
   or command grasshoppers to devour the countryside,
   or send an epidemic among my people.
[14] However, if my people, who are called by my name,
   will humble themselves,
   pray, search for me, and turn from their evil ways,
      then I will hear their prayer from heaven, forgive
         their sins,
   and heal their country.

—2 Chronicles 7:13-14

[2] "The Sun of Righteousness will rise with healing in his wings for you people who fear my name. You will go out and leap like calves let out of a stall.

—Malachi 4:2

## FOR DEEPER STUDY

*Read the following passages, considering the name* **PHYSICIAN** *and how its meaning relates to the context of the passage.*

Jeremiah 33:6–9     Matthew 8:5–10     Mark 9:17–29     Luke 17:11–17

John 4:46–54     Acts 5:12–16     2 Corinthians 12:7–10     James 5:14–16

# LAMB, LAMB OF GOD

## ἀρνίον ἀμνὸς τοῦ θεοῦ

### ARNION AMNOS TOU THEOU

Most of us picture lambs as downy white animals frolicking in rolling green meadows or carried tenderly in the arms of their shepherd. Lambs represent gentleness, purity, and innocence. Though it is one of the most tender images of Christ in the New Testament, the phrase "Lamb of God" would have conjured far more disturbing pictures to those who heard John the Baptist hail Jesus with these words. Hadn't many of them, at one time or another, carried one of their own lambs to the altar to be slaughtered as a sacrifice for their sins, a lamb that they had fed and bathed, the best animal in their small flock? Hadn't the bloody sacrifice of an innocent animal provided a vivid image of the consequences of transgressing the Mosaic law? Surely, John must have shocked his listeners by applying the phrase "Lamb of God" to a living man. When we pray to Jesus as the Lamb of God, we are praying to the One who voluntarily laid down his life to take in his own body the punishment for our sins and for the sins of the entire world.

## KEY SCRIPTURE

John saw **Yeshua** coming toward him the next day and said, "Look! This is the Lamb of God who takes away the sin of the world."

—John 1:29

# GOD REVEALS HIS NAME IN SCRIPTURE
## JOHN 1:29–34

*Open your personal Bible translation and read the same passages. Make note where you read the word* **LAMB**.

²⁹ John saw **Yeshua** coming toward him the next day and said, "Look! This is the Lamb of God who takes away the sin of the world. ³⁰ He is the one I spoke about when I said, 'A man who comes after me was before me because he existed before I did.' ³¹ I didn't know who he was. However, I came to baptize with water to show him to the people of Israel."

³² John said, "I saw the Spirit come down as a dove from heaven and stay on him. ³³ I didn't know who he was. But God, who sent me to baptize with water, had told me, 'When you see the Spirit come down and stay on someone, you'll know that person is the one who baptizes with the Holy Spirit.' ³⁴ I have seen this and have declared that this is the Son of God."

ἀρνίον
ἀμνὸς τοῦ θεοῦ

## UNDERSTANDING THE NAME

It is impossible to understand the title "**Lamb of God**" without understanding something about the practice of animal sacrifice in both Old and New Testaments. The sacrificial system provided a way for God's people to approach him even though they had violated the Mosaic law. When an animal was offered, its blood was shed, and its flesh was then burned on the altar. When the animal was completely consumed by fire, the sacrifice was called a "holocaust." When only part of the animal was burned, it was considered a "peace offering," intended to restore communion with God. The animal being sacrificed was a symbolic representation of the people's desire to offer their own lives to God.

To the Jews the lamb represented innocence and gentleness. Because the sacrifice was meant to represent the purity of intention of the person or people who offered it, lambs had to be without physical blemishes.

The New Testament uses two Greek words for Christ as "Lamb" or "Lamb of God": **Arnion** (AR-nee-on) and **Amnos tou Theou** (am-NOS tou the-OU). The phrase "Lamb of God" is found only in John's gospel, though Jesus is often referred to as "the Lamb" in the book of Revelation, where he is portrayed as the Lamb who, though slain, yet lives and reigns victorious. The New Testament also refers to Christ's followers as lambs.

## CONNECTING TO THE NAME

1. Jesus refused to defend himself when dragged before the Jewish leaders and before Pilate and Herod (Mark 14:53–65; 15:1–5). How does this relate to Isaiah 53:7? What does it say to you about Jesus?

2. What comes to your mind when you think of Jesus as the Lamb of God? How does Jesus as the Lamb of God relate to your life?

3. Do you struggle to let go of guilt over your sins or failures? How might this make it difficult to accept God's forgiveness?

4. Why is belonging to Jesus, the Lamb of God, the only security capable of preserving us from death?

5. Take a moment to close your eyes and lift your heart to Jesus, the Lamb. Now picture him alive again and standing next to God's throne in heaven. What do you see? What does he say? How do you respond?

## PRAYING A PASSAGE WITH GOD'S NAME

Ask God to increase your confidence in his forgiveness and confess any tendendy to identify yourself so closely with your sin that you have difficulty accepting God's forgiveness. Focus on the name **Amnos Tou Theou**, the **Lamb of God**, as you read 1 Peter 1:18–21.

> [18] Realize that you weren't set free from the worthless life handed down to you from your ancestors by a payment of silver or gold which can be destroyed. [19] Rather, the payment that freed you was the precious blood of Christ, the lamb with no defects or imperfections. [20] He is the lamb who was known long ago before the world existed, but for your good he became publicly known in the last period of time. [21] Through him you believe in God who brought Christ back to life and gave him glory. So your faith and confidence are in God.

## PRAYING THE NAME **LAMB OF GOD** FOR MYSELF

Look up and read: Genesis 22:6–13

Jesus was God's long-intended sacrifice for us. Read the passage below, which details Abraham's willingness to sacrifice his son, Isaac. Praise **Amnos Tou Theou** for being the perfect sacrifice that would set us free.

_____

_____

_____

_____

## PROMISES FROM THE **LAMB OF GOD**

They will never be hungry or thirsty again.
> Neither the sun nor any burning heat will ever overcome
> them.
[17] The lamb in the center near the throne will be their
> shepherd.
> He will lead them to springs filled with the water of life,
> and God will wipe every tear from their eyes."

—Revelation 7:16–17

[10] Then I heard a loud voice in heaven, saying,

"Now the salvation, power, kingdom of our God,
> and the authority of his Messiah have come.
> The one accusing our brothers and sisters,
> the one accusing them day and night in the presence of our God,
> has been thrown out.
[11] They won the victory over him because of the blood of the lamb
> and the word of their testimony.
> They didn't love their life so much that they refused to
> give it up.

—Revelation 12:10–11

## FOR DEEPER STUDY

*Read the following passages, considering the name* **LAMB OF GOD** *and how its meaning relates to the context of the passage.*

Exodus 12:1–23

Romans 8:31–36

1 Corinthians 5:7b

Revelation 17:12–14; 19:6–9; 21:9–14

# KING OF KINGS

## βασιλεὺς βασιλέων
### *BASILEUS BASILEON*

The world has never seen a king like Christ, a ruler mightier than any earthly sovereign and more powerful than the unseen powers of the universe. Though he entered the world humbly, as an infant born in Bethlehem, Magi from the east still recognized him as the newborn king. Though his reign unfolds in hidden ways, he has promised to come again, at which time he will reveal himself unambiguously as "King of Kings and Lord of Lords." When you pray to Jesus, the King of Kings, call to mind his mastery not only over human beings but over nature, disease, and death itself.

### KEY SCRIPTURE

On his clothes and his thigh he has a name written: King of Kings and Lord of Lords.

—Revelation 19:16

# GOD REVEALS HIS NAME IN SCRIPTURE
## REVELATION 19:11–16

*Open your personal Bible translation and read the same passage. Make note where you read* **KING OF KINGS**.

¹¹ I saw heaven standing open. There was a white horse, and its rider is named Faithful and True. With integrity he judges and wages war. ¹² His eyes are flames of fire. On his head are many crowns. He has a name written on him, but only he knows what it is. ¹³ He wears clothes dipped in blood, and his name is the Word of God.

¹⁴ The armies of heaven, wearing pure, white linen, follow him on white horses. ¹⁵ A sharp sword comes out of his mouth to defeat the nations. He will rule them with an iron scepter and tread the winepress of the fierce anger of God Almighty. ¹⁶ On his clothes and his thigh he has a name written: King of Kings and Lord of Lords.

βασιλεὺς βασιλέων

## UNDERSTANDING THE NAME

Today, Christ's kingdom unfolds in hidden ways as believers acknowledge him as King and Lord. But one day, when Christ comes again, his kingdom will be revealed as the greatest of all kingdoms. The passage from Revelation 19 presents Jesus riding not on a lowly donkey but on a magnificent white horse, as befits the greatest of all kings. Throughout the New Testament Jesus is variously referred to as "King," "King of the ages," "King of the Jews," "King of Israel," and "*King of Kings*"—this last one translated from the Greek phrase **Basileus Basileon** (bas-si-LEUS ba-si-LE-own). Even today some Christian churches are called "basilicas," a phrase meaning "the hall of the king."

# CONNECTING TO THE NAME

1. Write a list of qualities that describe the perfect king. Now compare and contrast these with the lives of some of today's rulers.

2. What do you think it means to have Jesus as your king? How have you experienced his reign in your life thus far?

3. How can we "seek first the kingdom of God" in the midst of our lives today (see Matthew 6:33)?

4. What would life on earth look like today if Jesus' reign was perfectly established?

5. How would your own life look if Jesus' reign was perfectly established in you?

# PRAYING A PASSAGE WITH GOD'S NAME

Focus on the name **Basileus Basileon**, "**King of Kings**," as you read Matthew 27:27–37. Reflect on how deep God's character reaches.

27 Then the governor's soldiers took **Yeshua** into the palace and gathered the whole troop around him. 28 They took off his clothes and put

a bright red cape on him. ²⁹ They twisted some thorns into a crown, placed it on his head, and put a stick in his right hand. They knelt in front of him and made fun of him by saying, "Long live the king of the Jews!" ³⁰ After they had spit on him, they took the stick and kept hitting him on the head with it.

³¹ After the soldiers finished making fun of **Yeshua**, they took off the cape and put his own clothes back on him. Then they led him away to crucify him.

³² On the way they found a man named Simon. He was from the city of Cyrene. The soldiers forced him to carry **Yeshua's** cross.

³³ They came to a place called Golgotha (which means "the place of the skull"). ³⁴ They gave him a drink of wine mixed with a drug called gall. When he tasted it, he refused to drink it. ³⁵ After they had crucified him, they divided his clothes among themselves by throwing dice. ³⁶ Then they sat there and kept watch over him. ³⁷ They placed a written accusation above his head. It read, "This is **Yeshua**, the king of the Jews."

## PRAYING THE NAME **KING OF KINGS** FOR MYSELF

Look up and read: Luke 17:22–25

Jesus was willing to be misunderstood for our salvation and rejected throughout history. In what ways do you think your generation has rejected **Basileus Basileon**? Have you rejected Jesus in any of these ways? Humble yourself and ask Jesus for the ability to see him and embrace him as he is, and not as you would have him be.

_____

_____

_____

_____

# PROMISES FROM THE **KING OF KINGS**

28 "And why worry about clothes? Notice how the flowers grow in the field. They never work or spin yarn for clothes. 29 But I say that not even Solomon in all his majesty was dressed like one of these flowers. 30 That's the way God clothes the grass in the field. Today it's alive, and tomorrow it's thrown into an incinerator. So how much more will he clothe you people who have so little faith?

31 "Don't ever worry and say, 'What are we going to eat?' or 'What are we going to drink?' or 32 Everyone is concerned about these things, and your heavenly Father certainly knows you need all of them. 33 But first, be concerned about his kingdom and what has his approval. Then all these things will be provided for you.

Matthew 6:28–33

## FOR DEEPER STUDY

*Read the following passages, considering the name* **KING OF KINGS** *and how its meaning relates to the context of the passage.*

Matthew 6:9–10; 25:31–43; 27:27–37

Luke 19:11–26

1 Corinthians 6:9–11

1 Timothy 6:11–16

2 Peter 1:5–11

Revelation 4; 11:15; 15:1–4; 17:12–14

# PRINCE OF PEACE

## שַׂר שָׁלוֹם

## *SAR SHALOM*

Who hasn't longed for peace, living in a world that is so often full of strife? The Hebrew word for peace, however, means much more than the absence of conflict or the end of turmoil. Shalom conveys not only a sense of tranquility but also of wholeness and completion. To enjoy shalom is to enjoy health, satisfaction, success, safety, well-being, and prosperity. Though the New Testament does not directly call Jesus the Prince of Peace, this title from Isaiah has traditionally been associated with him as the one who brings peace to the world.

Furthermore, Paul assured the Ephesian Christians saying of Jesus, "He himself is our peace" (Ephesians 2:14 NIV). When you pray to Sar Shalom, you are praying to Christ himself. To live in peace is to live in his presence.

## KEY SCRIPTURE

A child will be born for us.

A son will be given to us.

The government will rest on his shoulders.

He will be named:

Wonderful Counselor,

Mighty God,

Everlasting Father,

***Sar Shalom***.

—Isaiah 9:6

# GOD REVEALS HIS NAME IN SCRIPTURE
## ISAIAH 9:6; HEBREWS 13:20–21

*Open your personal Bible translation and read the same passage. Make note where* **SAR SHALOM** *is used as God's name.*

[6] A child will be born for us.

A son will be given to us.

The government will rest on his shoulders.

He will be named:

Wonderful Counselor,

Mighty God,

Everlasting Father,

***Sar Shalom***.

[20] The God of peace brought the great shepherd of the sheep, our Lord ***Yeshua***, back to life through the blood of an eternal promise. [21] May this God of peace prepare you to do every good thing he wants. May he work in us through ***Yeshua*** Christ to do what is pleasing to him. Glory belongs to ***Yeshua*** Christ forever. Amen.

## UNDERSTANDING THE NAME

Though the Hebrew title **Sar Shalom** (SAR sha-LOME) does not appear in the New Testament, the writer of Hebrews refers to he who God brought of himself, the God of peace. Both passages speak of a people being redeemed and saved by the One God sends in peace.

In Greek the word for peace is **eirene**. Like the Hebrew concept of shalom, the New Testament portrays peace as much more than the absence of conflict. The New Testament further develops our understanding of peace by revealing Jesus as the source of all peace. Though we were alienated from God because of our sins, Jesus reconciled us, making peace through his blood. Peace with God produces peace with others and peace within ourselves.

## CONNECTING TO THE NAME

1. What does the word "peace" mean to you? How does this differ from the biblical idea of shalom?

2. Why is the "Prince of Peace," *Sar Shalom*, a fitting title for Jesus? Can you think of incidents in his life that display his peace?

3. What was the ultimate work of peace by Jesus? How has Jesus become our peace?

4. Ask yourself whether you are experiencing Christ's peace in your life. How can you participate more deeply in his peace?

5. Are there relationships in your life that cause conflict and strife? How might you bring the peace of God into these relationships?

6. What do you think it means to walk in "the path of peace"?

## PRAYING A PASSAGE WITH GOD'S NAME

Praise Christ not only for making peace but for being our peace, for thoroughly transforming our lives with God, with others, and within ourselves. Focus on the name *Sar Shalom*, the "Prince of Peace," as you read Colossians 3:12–15.

[12] As holy people whom God has chosen and loved, be sympathetic, kind, humble, gentle, and patient. [13] Put up with each other, and forgive each other if anyone has a complaint. Forgive as the Lord forgave you. [14] Above all, be loving. This ties everything together perfectly. [15] Also, let Christ's peace control you. God has called you into this peace by bringing you into one body. Be thankful.

### *PRAYING THE NAME* **PRINCE OF PEACE** *FOR MYSELF*

Look up and read: Luke 19:41–44

All around us are threats to peace. Thank Sar Shalom for being peace itself. Humbly, ask him to address the circumstances that threaten peace in your heart, in your daily life, in your country, and in the world.

---

## PROMISES FROM THE **PRINCE OF PEACE**

> With perfect peace you will protect those whose minds
> cannot be changed,
>     because they trust you.
> —Isaiah 26:3

> I am *Yahweh* your *Elohim*.
>     I teach you what is best for you.
>     I lead you where you should go.
> <sup>18</sup> If only you had listened to my commands!
>     Your peace would be like a river that never runs dry.
>     Your righteousness would be like waves on the sea.
> —Isaiah 48:17-18

## FOR DEEPER STUDY

*Read the following passages, considering the name* **PRINCE OF PEACE**
*and how its meaning relates to the context of the passage.*

| | |
|---|---|
| Psalm 122:6–7 | Isaiah 32:17–18; 66:10–13 |
| Matthew 5:9 | John 14:23–27; 16:33; 20:19–20 |
| Romans 8:5–6 | Galatians 5:19–26 |
| Colossians 1:15–23 | |

# CHRIST, MESSIAH

## Χρίστος
### CHRISTOS

## מָשִׁיחַ
### MASHIACH

Most of us are so familiar with the title "Christ" that we tend to consider it part of Jesus' personal name. But what exactly does it mean? Like "Messiah," "Christ" means the "anointed one." The phrase "anointed one" refers to someone who has been set apart for a special mission. That was how the first Christians thought about Jesus. As Israel's Messiah, he was the greatest of all kings, the one called and empowered to destroy God's enemies and extend his kingdom throughout the earth. His mission was to put an end to our deepest troubles—to rebellion, sin, and death.

When we pray to Jesus Christ, we are praying to the Messiah, the Anointed One, whose mission involves calling the world back to God through the power of his love.

## KEY SCRIPTURE

"All the people of Israel should know beyond a doubt that God made Jesus, whom you crucified, both Lord and Christ."

—Acts 2:36

# GOD REVEALS HIS NAME IN SCRIPTURE
## ACTS 2:22–24, 32–33, 36–38

*Open your personal Bible translation and read the same passage. Make note where you read the name* **CHRIST**.

"Men of Israel, listen to what I say: **Yeshua** from Nazareth was a man whom God brought to your attention. You know that through this man God worked miracles, did amazing things, and gave signs. By using men who don't acknowledge Moses' Teachings, you crucified **Yeshua**, who was given over to death by a plan that God had determined in advance. But God brought him from death back to life and destroyed the pains of death, because death had no power to hold him."

"God brought this man **Yeshua** back to life. We are all witnesses to that. God used his power to give **Yeshua** the highest position. **Yeshua** has also received and has poured out the Holy Spirit as the Father had promised, and this is what you're seeing and hearing.

"All the people of Israel should know beyond a doubt that God made **Yeshua**, whom you crucified, both Lord and Christ."

When the people heard this, they were deeply upset. They asked Peter and the other apostles, "Brothers, what should we do?"

Peter answered them, "All of you must turn to God and change the way you think and act, and each of you must be baptized in the name of **Yeshua** Christ so that your sins will be forgiven. Then you will receive the Holy Spirit as a gift.

## UNDERSTANDING THE NAME

Many ancient peoples believed that oil rubbed onto the body could impart strength, health, and beauty. Since oil was a staple of life in biblical times, used for lighting, cooking, medicine, cosmetic purposes, hygiene, and hospitality, it served as a symbol of both wealth and joy. An abundance of oil was evidence of God's pleasure; scarcity symbolized his displeasure.

Oil was also used for sacred purposes, such as consecrating altars and vessels for worship, indicating that they had been set apart for the Lord's purposes. People could also be anointed and set apart. Though some of Israel's high priests were anointed when they took office, Israel's kings, especially those descended from David, were anointed rather than crowned. According to rabbinic tradition, oil (olive oil mixed with spices like cinnamon, calamus, and myrrh) was poured on their heads in a circle to form a crown. This anointing signified the king's right to rule. It meant that God had blessed him with authority, strength, and honor.

When the prophet Samuel anointed David as king, David was also given the gift of the Spirit and accorded the Lord's special protection.

In time, oil became a symbol for the Holy Spirit, who imparts divine favor, power, and protection. The English word "christen" ("to anoint") comes from the Greek verb chrio ("to anoint"). The New Testament identifies Jesus as Christ, the "Anointed One," no less than 530 times. Jesus, however, was not anointed with oil but with the Holy Spirit at his baptism in the Jordan River. The early Christians understood that Jesus was the Christ—the Messiah, or *Mashiach* (ma-SHEE-ach)—in a unique sense. Like no king before him, he was called to heal the rift between God and his people.

Christ fulfilled his mission as the ideal king in a completely unexpected way, confounding his contemporaries, who expected the Messiah to be a powerful earthly king who would deliver Israel from its enemies. In order to avoid being forced into playing this political role, Jesus avoided the title of Christ or Messiah throughout most of his life. Finally, shortly before his death, he answered the high priest's question: "Are you the Christ, the Son of the Blessed One?" with the startling confession: "I am."

# CONNECTING TO THE NAME

1. Describe in your own words what it means to say that Jesus was anointed, or set apart for God's service.

2. Why do you think the Acts 2 passage speaks about the need for repentance and being baptized in the name of Jesus Christ? What has your repentance and baptism meant to you? To God?

3. What do you think it means to receive the gift of the Holy Spirit?

4. Why were the people who were listening to Jesus deeply upset? When have you experienced being deeply upset or "cut to the heart" as the NIV puts it, by who the Messiah is and what he has done for you?

5. What do you think it means for believers to be anointed or set apart for Christ's service? How have you experienced this anointing in your own life?

# PRAYING A PASSAGE WITH GOD'S NAME

Thank God for giving you the gift of faith in his Son, Jesus Christ. Focus on the name *Christos*, "Christ" or "Messiah," as you read Matthew 16:15–17.

[15] He asked them, "But who do you say I am?"

[16] Simon Peter answered, "You are the Messiah, the Son of the living God!"

[17] **Yeshua** replied, "Simon, son of Jonah, you are blessed! No human revealed this to you, but my Father in heaven revealed it to you.

> **Praise God:** Because his thoughts are higher than ours.
> **Offer Thanks:** For Christ's willingness to suffer.
> **Confess:** Any tendency to settle for less than what Christ desires for you.
> **Ask God:** To give you his mind and heart.

## PRAYING THE NAME **CHRIST** FOR MYSELF

Look up and read: 1 Peter 4:12–19

Sharing in the suffering of Christos can feel humiliating and painful. In what "strange" ways have you been asked to share in Christ's suffering? Ask him for the grace to see these sufferings as a privilege because of your close connection to him.

_____

_____

_____

_____

# PROMISES FROM **CHRIST**, OUR **MESSIAH**

[18] You can depend on God. Our message to you isn't false; it's true. [19] God's Son, **Yeshua** Christ, whom I, Silvanus, and Timothy told you about, was true not false. Because of him our message was always true. [20] Certainly, Christ made God's many promises come true. For that reason, because of our message, people also honor God by saying, "Amen!"

[21] God establishes us, together with you, in a relationship with Christ. He has also anointed us. [22] In addition, he has put his seal of ownership on us and has given us the Spirit as his guarantee.

2 Corinthians 1:18–22

[20] But now Christ has come back from the dead. He is the very first person of those who have died to come back to life. [21] Since a man brought death, a man also brought life back from death. [22] As everyone dies because of Adam, so also everyone will be made alive because of Christ.

—1 Corinthians 15:20–22

## FOR DEEPER STUDY

*Read the following passages, considering the name* **CHRIST** *and how its meaning relates to the context of the passage.*

| | | |
|---|---|---|
| Isaiah 52:13–15 | Luke 24:45–48 | John 12:1–7 |
| Romans 8:32–37 | 2 Corinthians 12:7–10 | Galatians 3:26–28 |
| Philippians 2:5–11 | | |

# RABBI, RABBOUNI, TEACHER

## ῥαββί, ῥαββουνί
### RHABB RHABBOUNI

## διδάσκαλος
### DIDASKALOS

In Jesus' day, the name "rabbi" or "teacher" was normally reserved for someone who had studied under another rabbi for many years. Jesus offended the religious leaders of his day by ignoring this system. Instead of apprenticing himself to a rabbi, he simply laid down his carpenter tools and called twelve ordinary men to become his disciples. Unlike other rabbis, who merely passed on the teaching of the rabbi under whom they had studied, Jesus spoke with an authority that startled many of his listeners.

Two thousand years later, we are called to become his disciples, to stay as close to him as a disciple would to a rabbi, studying his life, examining his teaching, and allowing his Spirit to remake us in his image. When you pray to Rabbi Jesus, remember that you are praying to the only Teacher who is all-wise, all-good, and all-powerful, able to transform not only your mind but also your heart.

## KEY SCRIPTURE

But don't make others call you Rabbi, because you have only one teacher, and you are all followers.

—Matthew 23:8

# GOD REVEALS HIS NAME IN SCRIPTURE
## MATTHEW 23:8; JOHN 13:6–8, 12–15

*Open your personal Bible translation and read the same passage. Make note where you read the name* **RABBI** *or* **TEACHER***.*

⁸ But don't make others call you Rabbi, because you have only one teacher, and you are all followers.

⁶ When **Yeshua** came to Simon Peter, Peter asked him, "Lord, are you going to wash my feet?"

⁷ **Yeshua** answered Peter, "You don't know now what I'm doing. You will understand later."

⁸ Peter told **Yeshua**, "You will never wash my feet."

**Yeshua** replied to Peter, "If I don't wash you, you don't belong to me."

¹² After **Yeshua** had washed their feet and put on his outer clothes, he took his place at the table again. Then he asked his disciples, "Do you understand what I've done for you? ¹³ You call me teacher and Lord, and you're right because that's what I am. ¹⁴ So if I, your Lord and teacher, have washed your feet, you must wash each other's feet. ¹⁵ I've given you an example that you should follow.

# διδάσκαλος

## UNDERSTANDING THE NAME

In the first century, "Rabbi" (ra-BEE, a Hebrew word) was used as a term of respect for teachers of the Scriptures. After AD 70 it became formalized as a title for scribes and theologians trained in the law. (*Rabbouni* [ra-BOU-nee] is an expanded Hebrew form that means "my rabbi.") Scribes were also known as "teachers of the law." The King James Version of the Bible calls them "lawyers."

"Rabbi" is literally translated "my great one" and can also be translated as "my master" or "my teacher." During the first century it was customary for a rabbi to take disciples, who would be bound to him for life. After spending several years with their rabbi studying Scripture and the oral and written traditions surrounding it, the disciples would in turn become rabbis through the laying on of hands.

Another word for teacher in the New Testament is the Greek word *didaskalos* (di-DAS-ka-los). Jesus was an enormously popular teacher who drew crowds wherever he went, using questions, discussions, proverbs, symbolic actions, parables, and even miracles in order to teach people the way to live. The content of his teaching is most powerfully and eloquently evident in the story of his life.

# ῥαββί, ῥαββουνί

## CONNECTING TO THE NAME

1. Why do you think Jesus cautioned his disciples in Matthew 23:8 against the title "rabbi?"

2. Why do you think Jesus washed his disciples' feet the night before his death, making this one of the last lessons he would teach them prior to his crucifixion?

3.  Describe ways in which you have experienced people in leadership serving you.

4.  How might God be calling you to serve in humble and hidden ways?

5.  In Luke 6:40 Jesus said, "A student is not above his teacher, but everyone who is fully trained will be like his teacher." To whom do you look for counsel, guidance, and leadership? Whom do you work to emulate?

6.  Do you avoid or resist certain difficult teachings of Christ? What are they?

7.  How would your life be different if you understood that your primary identity consisted of being a disciple of Rabbi Jesus?

# PRAYING A PASSAGE WITH GOD'S NAME

Focus on the meaning of the name *Rhabb, Rhabbouni, Didaskalos,* "Rabbi," "My Rabbi," "Teacher," as you read John 3:1–4, 11–12.

¹ Nicodemus was a Pharisee and a member of the Jewish council. ² He came to **Jesus** one night and said to him, "Rabbi, we know that God has sent you as a teacher. No one can perform the miracles you perform unless God is with him."

³ **Yeshua** replied to Nicodemus, "I can guarantee this truth: No one can see the kingdom of God without being born from above."

⁴ Nicodemus asked him, "How can anyone be born when he's an old man? He can't go back inside his mother a second time to be born, can he?"

¹¹ I can guarantee this truth: We know what we're talking about, and we confirm what we've seen. Yet, you don't accept our message. ¹² If you don't believe me when I tell you about things on earth, how will you believe me when I tell you about things in heaven?

## PRAYING THE NAME **RABBI** FOR MYSELF

Look up and read: Matthew 13:31–32

One of the things that we are taught by Jesus is that things are often not what they seem. The smallest seed grows into the largest tree. What has Jesus taught you to see differently? What did you see before you began to follow Jesus? What did you see after?

# PROMISES FROM **JESUS**, OUR **RABBI**

[5] "Now I'm going to the one who sent me. Yet, none of you asks me where I'm going. [6] But because I've told you this, you're filled with sadness. [7] However, I am telling you the truth: It's good for you that I'm going away. If I don't go away, the helper won't come to you.

[12] "I have a lot more to tell you, but that would be too much for you now. [13] When the Spirit of Truth comes, he will guide you into the full truth. He won't speak on his own. He will speak what he hears and will tell you about things to come. [14] He will give me glory, because he will tell you what I say. [15] Everything the Father says is also what I say. That is why I said, 'He will take what I say and tell it to you.'

—John 16:5-7, 12-15

## FOR DEEPER STUDY

*Read the following passages, considering the name* **RABBI** *or* **TEACHER** *and how its meaning relates to the context of the passage.*

Psalm 119:18

Matthew 19:16–21; 22:36–40; 23:8–12; 26:48–50

John 9:1–3; 12:23–26

1 Corinthians 1:25

2 Timothy 3:16

James 1:5

# WORD

## λόγος
## LOGOS

Though God has always revealed himself in some way, the incarnation is the clearest, most compelling revelation of who God is—of his holiness, love, and power. Because Jesus is one with the Father, he is uniquely able to communicate God's heart and mind. As Logos, or "the Word," everything about Jesus—his teaching, miracles, suffering, death, and resurrection—speaks to us of God. Our destiny depends on how well we listen. Will we believe, or will we turn a deaf ear to the message of God's love? When you pray to Jesus as the Word, you are praying to the one whose voice calls us from death to life and from darkness to light.

## KEY SCRIPTURE

The Word became human and lived among us. We saw his glory. It was the glory that the Father shares with his only Son, a glory full of kindness and truth.

—John 1:14

# GOD REVEALS HIS NAME IN SCRIPTURE
## JOHN 1:1–3, 10–14

*Open your personal Bible translation and read the same passage. Make note where you read the name* **WORD**.

In the beginning the Word already existed. The Word was with God, and the Word was God. He was already with God in the beginning.

Everything came into existence through him. Not one thing that exists was made without him.

He was in the world, and the world came into existence through him. Yet, the world didn't recognize him. He went to his own people, and his own people didn't accept him. However, he gave the right to become God's children to everyone who believed in him. These people didn't become God's children in a physical way—from a human impulse or from a husband's desire to have a child. They were born from God.

The Word became human and lived among us. We saw his glory. It was the glory that the Father shares with his only Son, a glory full of kindness and truth.

## UNDERSTANDING THE NAME

John's gospel begins by calling Jesus the Logos (LO-gos), the "Word." Though Logos was a term used in Greek philosophy, John echoes a Hebrew mindset by using it to refer not to a rational principle or an impersonal force but to the one who created the universe by speaking it into existence. Unlike the prophets, who merely spoke God's word, Jesus is God's dynamic, creative, life-giving Word.

Furthermore, John says, "The Word became flesh and made his dwelling among us" (John 1:14 NIV). The Greek for "made his dwelling" is linked to the word for "tent" or "tabernacle." Jewish readers would have immediately recognized this as a reference to the Tent of Meeting, in which God's glory dwelt prior to the building of the temple in Jerusalem. Jesus, the Word made flesh, became a man so that through his miracles, teachings, and way of life we could perceive God's glory. He is the Word calling out to us, healing our deafness and bringing us back to God.

No wonder Jesus responded to Philip by saying: "Don't you know me, Philip, even after I have been among you such a long time? Anyone who has seen me has seen the Father. How can you say, 'Show us the Father'? Don't you believe that I am in the Father, and that the Father is in me?" (John 14:9–10 NIV). We are to respond to Jesus, the Word, with both faith and faithfulness, reproducing Christ's life so that the Word may become flesh in us.

## CONNECTING TO THE NAME

1. Compare Genesis 1:1–5 with John 1:1–5. Why do you think John begins his gospel this way?

2. John says that though the world came into existence through him, the world did not recognize him. Do you think this is still true today? Why or why not?

3. John writes, "he [the Word] gave the right to become God's children to everyone who believed in him." How does being a son or daughter of God shape the way you see yourself?

4. How hungry are you for the Word of God as spoken in the Bible? How do you express its value to you?

# PRAYING A PASSAGE WITH GOD'S NAME

Praise God for creating everything through his all-powerful Word. Ask the Lord to open your ears to hear what he is saying. Focus on the name *Logos*, the "Word," as you read Psalm 33:6–9.

The heavens were made by the word of **Yahweh**

and all the stars by the breath of his mouth.

⁷ He gathers the water in the sea like a dam

and puts the oceans in his storehouses.

⁸ Let all the earth fear **Yahweh**.

Let all who live in the world stand in awe of him.

⁹ He spoke, and it came into being.

He gave the order, and there it stood.

## PRAYING THE NAME THE **WORD** FOR MYSELF

Look up and read: 1 Thessalonians 2:13

Human words absolutely fail us, but the Logos enriches us and actually dwells within us. Is there anything that holds you back from believing that God's **Word** is truly his word, and therefore completely different than human words? Ask God to show you the truth of his **Word**.

_____

_____

_____

_____

# PROMISES FROM THE **WORD**

[27] While **Yeshua** was speaking, a woman in the crowd shouted, "How blessed is the mother who gave birth to you and the breasts that nursed you."

[28] **Yeshua** replied, "Rather, how blessed are those who hear and obey God's word."

Luke 11:27–28

[22] Do what God's word says. Don't merely listen to it, or you will fool yourselves. [23] If someone listens to God's word but doesn't do what it says, he is like a person who looks at his face in a mirror, [24] studies his features, goes away, and immediately forgets what he looks like. [25] However, the person who continues to study God's perfect laws that make people free and who remains committed to them will be blessed. People like that don't merely listen and forget; they actually do what God's laws say.

—James 1:22–25

## FOR DEEPER STUDY

*Read the following passages, considering the name the* **WORD** *and how its meaning relates to the context of the passage.*

| | | | |
|---|---|---|---|
| Psalm 119:105 | Isaiah 55:10–11 | Matthew 4:1–4 | Mark 8:38; 13:31 |
| Luke 8:4–15 | John 5:24–26 | 2 Timothy 4:1–5 | Hebrews 1:1–4 |
| Revelation 19:11–15 | | | |

# CORNER-STONE, CAPSTONE

## ἀκρογωνιαῖος λίθος
### AKROGONIAIOS LITHOS

In the ancient world, stones were used for building altars, homes, palaces, and temples. When "capstone" or "cornerstone" is mentioned in the Bible, it refers to a particularly important stone that held two rows of stones together in a corner, one that stabilized the structure at the foundation, or a stone that formed the keystone over an arch or at the top of a roof parapet. In order to hold the structure together, the cornerstone had to be perfectly fitted for the task, both strong and well shaped. A flawed or poorly cut stone would compromise the building's integrity.

Jesus is the Cornerstone or Capstone to which we are joined as living stones. Together we form a spiritual house in which God can dwell. As the foundation stone on which God is building his kingdom, Jesus is strong

enough to hold everything together. He is also the fitting conclusion to all God's work. When you pray to him as the Cornerstone, you are praying to the one on whom you can base your life.

## KEY SCRIPTURE

Then **Yeshua** looked straight at them and asked, "What, then, does this Scripture verse mean:

'The stone that the builders rejected
has become the cornerstone'?
—Luke 20:17

# GOD REVEALS HIS NAME IN SCRIPTURE
## LUKE 20:9–18

*Open your personal Bible translation and read the same passage. Make note where you read the name* **CORNERSTONE**.

9 Then, using this illustration, **Yeshua** spoke to the people: "A man planted a vineyard, leased it to vineyard workers, and went on a long trip.

10 "At the right time he sent a servant to the workers to obtain from them a share of the grapes from the vineyard. But the workers beat the servant and sent him back with nothing. 11 So he sent a different servant. The workers beat him, treated him shamefully, and sent him back with nothing. 12 Then he sent a third servant. But they injured this one and threw him out of the vineyard.

13 "Then the owner of the vineyard said, 'What should I do? I'll send my son, whom I love. They'll probably respect him.'

14 "When the workers saw him, they talked it over among themselves. They said, 'This is the heir. Let's kill him so that the inheritance will be ours.' 15 So they threw him out of the vineyard and killed him.

"What will the owner of the vineyard do to them? 16 He will destroy these workers and give the vineyard to others."

Those who heard him said, "That's unthinkable!"

17 Then **Yeshua** looked straight at them and asked, "What, then, does this Scripture verse mean:

'The stone that the builders rejected
has become the cornerstone'?

18 Everyone who falls on that stone will be broken. If that stone falls on anyone, it will crush that person."

## UNDERSTANDING THE NAME

When Jesus quoted the passage from Psalm 118:22, referring to the stone the builders rejected, he was pointing to his rejection by the Jewish nation and its leaders. Despite their rejection, God's purposes could not be thwarted. In fact, the Master Builder would make Jesus, through his death and resurrection, the Akrogoniaios Lithos (ah-kro-go-nee-EYE-os LI-thos), capstone or cornerstone, on which he would build his church. The New Testament portrays the whole community of believers as a holy temple in which God dwells. To those who reject Jesus and his saving message, he will be not a cornerstone but a stone of stumbling, because rejection of God's chosen one inevitably brings judgment. As an interesting side note, a royal name was often inscribed on the cornerstone, and among the ancient Canaanites before the time of Joshua, the laying of the foundation stone may sometimes have been accompanied by human sacrifice. Tragically, a number of skeletons, especially those of small babies in earthen jars, have been found at various sites. Whether these remains were from children who had died natural deaths or from those who were sacrificed is difficult to tell.

## CONNECTING TO THE NAME

1. Why do you think Jesus' comments about "the stone the builders rejected" immediately follow the parable of the vineyard?

2. Give an example from our day of how people stumble over Jesus and find him a rock of offence.

3. What do you think it means to build your life on Jesus as the Cornerstone? Give some examples from your own life.

4. How does basing your life on Jesus enable you to stand rather than collapse during times of unbearable pressure?

5. Which of your priorities need to shift in order for you to stand more squarely on Christ rather than trying to "stand" on insecure foundations like money, success, intelligence, relationships?

6. Picture yourself as a living stone being built into a spiritual house. How might this image affect your relationship with others in the church?

## PRAYING A PASSAGE WITH GOD'S NAME

Praise Jesus for being the cornerstone of the church. Thank him for the privilege of becoming part of the temple he is building. Focus on the name *Akrogoniaios Lithos*, the "Cornerstone" or "Capstone," as you read Matthew 24:1–2.

As **Yeshua** left the temple courtyard and was walking away, his disciples came to him. They proudly pointed out to him the temple buildings. [2] **Yeshua** said to them, "You see all these buildings, don't you? I can guarantee this truth: Not one of these stones will be left on top of another. Each one will be torn down."

## PRAYING IN THE NAME "CORNERSTONE" FOR MYSELF

Look up and read: Isaiah 8:13-14. Jesus is a place of safety for us. Ask him for the grace to be able to build your life on him, even through times of confusion and contradiction.

_____

_____

_____

_____

Christ tells us that we can build an impossible to collapse house by hearing what he says and obeying it. Take a moment to ask the Holy Spirit what kind of house you are building. Describe any chinks in the foundation that he may reveal.

Matthew 7:24–27

_____

_____

_____

_____

## PROMISES FROM **JESUS**, OUR **CORNERSTONE**

[16] This is what **Adonay Yahweh** says:

> I am going to lay a rock in Zion,
>      a rock that has been tested,
>      a precious cornerstone,
>      a solid foundation.
>           Whoever believes in him will not worry.
> —Isaiah 28:16

That is why Scripture says, "I am laying a precious cornerstone in Zion, and the person who believes in him will never be ashamed."

—1 Peter 2:6

## FOR DEEPER STUDY

*Read the following passages, considering the name* **CORNERSTONE** *or* **CAPSTONE** *and how its meaning relates to the context of the passage.*

Psalm 127:1

Luke 19:41–44

John 2:13–20

Acts 3:1–8; 4:5–12

Romans 9:30–32

1 Corinthians 3:11

Ephesians 2:19–22

# BRIGHT MORNING STAR

## ἀστὴρ λαμπρὸς πρωϊνός

### ASTER LAMPROS PROINOS

In the last chapter of Revelation, Jesus calls himself the "bright morning star." In ancient times, the morning star was thought of as a herald of the new day, signaling the dawn of hope and joy. The brightest object in the sky aside from the sun and moon, it is a fitting type for Christ, who ushers in a new day for the entire world. When you call on Jesus, the bright morning star, you are calling on the one from whom all darkness flees.

## KEY SCRIPTURE

"I, *Yeshua*, have sent my angel to give this testimony to you for the churches. I am the root and descendant of David. I am the bright morning star."

—Revelation 22:16

## GOD REVEALS HIS NAME IN SCRIPTURE
### REVELATION 22:14–16

*Open your personal Bible translation and read the same passage. Make note where you read the name* **STAR**.

"Blessed are those who wash their robes so that they may have the right to the tree of life and may go through the gates into the city. Outside are dogs, sorcerers, sexual sinners, murderers, idolaters, and all who lie in what they say and what they do.

"I, *Yeshua*, have sent my angel to give this testimony to you for the churches. I am the root and descendant of David. I am the bright morning star."

# ἀστὴρ λαμπρὸς

## UNDERSTANDING THE NAME

What the Bible refers to as the morning star is actually the planet Venus, known since prehistoric times. As the second planet from the sun, it is also one of the hottest. A relatively young planet, it is Earth's closest neighbor and is often called our sister planet. Because of its appearance in the eastern sky before dawn, it was thought of as the harbinger of sunrise. The title *Aster Lampros Proinos* (as-TAIR lam-PROS pro-i-NOS) presents a powerful and beautiful image of the one who is also known as "the Light of the World."

# πρωϊνός

# CONNECTING TO THE NAME

1. Jesus says he is coming soon. In what ways do you think his second coming will differ from his first?

2. Describe your attitude toward the second coming — fear, doubt, hope, joy? Why do you feel the way you do?

3. What kinds of people is Jesus describing in the passage from Revelation?

4. Throughout time, stars have been used by travelers as reference points. How does Jesus function as a reference point, our guiding star?

5. The writer to the Hebrews tells us to "fix our eyes on Jesus" (Hebrews 12:2). How will fixing your eyes on Jesus make a difference at times of adversity, confusion, fear, or temptation?

6. Stars shine in the darkness of night, but the morning star announces a new day. How does Jesus, the Bright Morning Star, announce the dawn of a new day in your life and in the world?

## PRAYING A PASSAGE WITH GOD'S NAME

Praise God for keeping his promise by sending his Son to light our path as he gives hope to the world. Focus on the name *Aster Lampros Proinos*, the "Bright Morning Star," as you read Numbers 24:17.

> I see someone who is not here now.
> I look at someone who is not nearby.
> A star will come from Jacob.
> A scepter will rise from Israel.
> He will crush the heads of the Moabites
> and destroy all the people of Sheth.

### PRAYING THE NAME **BRIGHT MORNING STAR** FOR MYSELF

Look up and read: 2 Peter 1:16–19

Peter speaks of Jesus as a morning star and as a voice. Is the voice of *Aster Lampros Proinos* clear in your life, like a star on a cloudless night? Or do you have trouble hearing from him? Ask Jesus for the grace to see him and to hear his voice.

_____

_____

_____

_____

# PROMISES FROM THE
# BRIGHT MORNING STAR

If I say, "Let the darkness hide me
    and let the light around me turn into night,"
[12] even the darkness is not too dark for you.
    Night is as bright as day.
        Darkness and light are the same to you.
    —Psalm 139:11–12

When that day comes, the deaf will hear the words written in
the book.
    The blind will see out of their gloom and darkness.
[19] Humble people again will find joy in **Yahweh**.
    The poorest of people will find joy in **Qedosh Yisrael**.
    —Isaiah 29:18–19

## FOR DEEPER STUDY

*Read the following passages, considering the name* **BRIGHT MORNING STAR** *and how its meaning relates to the context of the passage.*

Matthew 2:1–1; 16:2–3

Luke 1:67–79

# LION OF THE TRIBE OF JUDAH

## λέων ἐκ τῆς φυλῆς Ἰούδα

### LEON EK TES PHYLES IOUDA

Only once in the New Testament is Jesus described as a lion. The book of Revelation (named in part for what it reveals about Christ) portrays the risen Jesus as the only one worthy to open the scroll that contains the ultimate unfolding of God's purposes for the world.

The apostle John perceived Jesus as both Lion and Lamb, who through his death and resurrection becomes the ultimate victor and conqueror. When you pray to Jesus as the Lion of the Tribe of Judah, you are praying to the one with the power to banish all fear, to the one who watches over you with his fierce protecting love. You are also praying to the one who is judge of the living and the dead.

## KEY SCRIPTURE

I cried bitterly because no one was found who deserved to open the scroll or look inside it.

Then one of the leaders said to me, "Stop crying! The Lion from the tribe of Judah, the Root of David, has won the victory. He can open the scroll and the seven seals on it."

—Revelation 5:4–5

# GOD REVEALS HIS NAME IN SCRIPTURE
## GENESIS 49:8–10, REVELATION 5:5

*Open your personal Bible translation and read the same passages. Make note where you read the name* **JUDAH** *or* **LION***.*

8 "***Judah***, your brothers will praise you.
Your hand will be on the neck of your enemies.
Your father's sons will bow down to you.
9 Judah, you are a lion cub.
You have come back from the kill, my son.
He lies down and rests like a lion.
He is like a lioness. Who dares to disturb him?
10 A scepter will never depart from Judah
nor a ruler's staff from between his feet
until Shiloh comes
and the people obey him.

5 Then one of the leaders said to me, "Stop crying! The Lion from the tribe of Judah, the Root of David, has won the victory. He can open the scroll and the seven seals on it."

# λέων ἐκ τῆς φυλῆς Ἰούδα

## UNDERSTANDING THE NAME

Throughout the Bible, the lion appears as a symbol of might, and it is hardly surprising that Israel's enemies are sometimes depicted as lions. In the New Testament, Peter calls the devil a roaring lion and warns believers that he is constantly on the prowl, looking for someone to devour.

Though lions are sometimes a symbol of evil, they are also used as symbols of God's people. Near the end of his life, the patriarch Jacob prayed a blessing over his twelve sons. When it came time to bless Judah, he compared him to a lion—hence the phrase "the Lion of the Tribe of Judah" (***Aryeh Lammatteh Yehudah*** in Hebrew, pronounced ar-YEH la-mat-TEH ye-hou-DAH, or ***Leon ek tes Phyles Iouda***, in Greek, pronounced LE-own ek teys fu-LAIS YOU-dah). Jacob's prediction that the scepter would not depart from Judah has been traditionally applied to the Messiah.

In the Hebrew Scriptures, Yahweh is sometimes depicted as a lion who roars in judgment against the nations and against his own faithless people. But he is also depicted as a mighty lion who fights fiercely on behalf of his people. Revelation depicts the risen Christ as the mightiest of all victors. He is the Lion of the Tribe of Judah, the one found worthy to open the scrolls of history; this means that he is in charge of history and of how the world's destiny unfolds.

## CONNECTING TO THE NAME

1. Why do you think the book of Revelation portrays Jesus as both Lion and Lamb?

2. In the Bible "seven" is considered a sacred number, symbolizing perfection or completeness, while a "horn" symbolizes power. What does this say to you about how the Lamb is portrayed in Revelation 5?

3. How have you experienced and understood both the "lamblike" and "lionlike" nature of Jesus in your own life?

4. What does it mean for us "to be a kingdom and priests to serve our God"?

5. The Lion of the Tribe of Judah, the ultimate victor and conqueror, has the power to banish all fear and to watch over you with fierce, protective love. Picture this literally, then describe how this promise of safety might affect the way you face your fears.

6. What specific victories has the Lion of Judah already won in your life?

7. If you could choose one adjective to describe the passage from Revelation 5, what would it be and why? Would you call it bizarre, moving, perplexing, enlightening, or something else?

## PRAYING A PASSAGE WITH GOD'S NAME

Focus on the name *Aryeh Lammatteh Yehudah*, "Lion of the Tribe of Judah" as you read Hosea 11:8–11.

> "How can I give you up, Ephraim?
>> How can I hand you over, Israel?
>> How can I make you like Admah?
>> How can I treat you like Zeboim?
>> I have changed my mind.
>>> I am deeply moved.
> ⁹ I will not act on my burning anger.
>> I will not destroy Ephraim again.
>> I am **El**, not a human.
>> I am the Holy One among you,
>> and I will not come to you in anger.
>
> ¹⁰ "My people will follow **Yahweh** when I roar like a lion.
>> When I roar, my children will come trembling from the
>>> west.
> ¹¹ They will come trembling like birds from Egypt
>> and like doves from Assyria.
>> I will settle them in their own homes,"
>>> declares **Yahweh**.

### PRAYING THE NAME LION OF THE TRIBE OF JUDAH
### FOR MYSELF

Look up and read: Isaiah 11:6–9

Jesus is the lion and the lamb, who will bring all things to reconciliation at the end of history. Tell him about anything or any circumstance that feels irreconcilable, and write a prayer of praise, surrendering that circumstance to him.

---

## PROMISES FROM THE
# LION OF THE TRIBE OF JUDAH

"Be strong and courageous. Don't tremble! Don't be afraid of them! **Yahweh** your **Elohim** is the one who is going with you. He won't abandon you or leave you."
—Deuteronomy 31:6

A wicked person flees when no one is chasing him,
but righteous people are as bold as lions.
—Proverbs 28:1

### FOR DEEPER STUDY

*Read the following passages, considering the name the* **LION OF THE TRIBE OF JUDAH** *and how its meaning relates to the context of the passage.*

Psalm 106:8

Proverbs 19:12

Amos 3:6–8

Joel 3:16

# LORD

## κύριος
## KYRIOS

Christianity's earliest confession of faith consisted of three short but incredibly powerful words: Jesus is Lord! The early Christians believed that the Father had placed Jesus, by virtue of his death and resurrection, at the apex of time and eternity—higher than any power or person in the universe. It is no wonder that Paul was "convinced that neither death nor life, neither angels nor demons, neither the present nor the future, nor any powers, neither height nor depth, nor anything else in all creation, will be able to separate us from the love of God that is in Christ Jesus our Lord" (Romans 8:38–39 NIV). Both those who love him and those who oppose him will one day call Jesus "Lord." In the end, even the devil will be forced to acknowledge him.

As you bow your head in prayer before the sovereign Lord, remember that you are placing your life—the worst of your disappointments, the most protracted of your struggles, the wildest of your dreams—squarely in his hands. Knowing Jesus as Lord will lead you to a deeper experience of his presence and his power.

## KEY SCRIPTURE

This is why God has given him an exceptional honor—
the name honored above all other names—
so that at the name of **Yeshua** everyone in heaven, on earth,
and in the world below will kneel
and confess that **Yeshua** Christ is Lord
to the glory of God the Father.
—Philippians 2:9–11

# GOD REVEALS HIS NAME IN SCRIPTURE
## PHILIPPIANS 2:5–11

*Open your personal Bible translation and read the same passage. Make note where you read the name* **LORD**.

⁵ Have the same attitude that Christ **Yeshua** had.

⁶ Although he was in the form of God and equal with God,
he did not take advantage of this equality.
⁷ Instead, he emptied himself by taking on the form of a
servant,
by becoming like other humans,
by having a human appearance.
⁸ He humbled himself by becoming obedient to the point of
death,
death on a cross.
⁹ This is why God has given him an exceptional honor—
the name honored above all other names—
¹⁰ so that at the name of **Yeshua** everyone in heaven, on
earth,
and in the world below will kneel
¹¹ and confess that **Yeshua** Christ is Lord
to the glory of God the Father.

## UNDERSTANDING THE NAME

The Greek word **Kyrios** (KU-ree-os) is used in the New Testament to refer to an owner, emperor, king, father, husband, or master. It can also translate three Hebrew names and titles of God: *Yahweh*, Adonay, and Elohim. When people addressed Jesus as **Kyrios** or "Lord" in the Gospels, they were often simply showing respect to him as a rabbi or teacher, addressing him as "sir" rather than acknowledging him as the Lord God. But after his death and resurrection, the title "Lord" began to be widely used by believers in a more specialized sense.

Remember the apostle Thomas, who at first doubted accounts of Christ's resurrection? When Jesus appeared to him after his death, Thomas instinctively responded with a confession of faith, saying: "My Lord and my God!" (John 20:28). Over time, the title "Lord" began to take on the characteristics of a name. As such, it clearly identifies Jesus with *Yahweh*, the covenant name of God in the Hebrew Scriptures. Of the 717 passages in which **Kyrios** occurs in the New Testament, the majority are found in Luke's gospel, the Book of Acts, and Paul's writings.

## CONNECTING TO THE NAME

1. How did God the Father respond to Jesus' willing obedience, even to death on a cross?

2. What do you think it means that every tongue will confess that Jesus Christ is Lord?

3. How does God's idea of greatness differ from the usual definition?

4. Have you been reserving any part of your life—a relationship, habit, dream, or concern—because you fear what the Lord may ask of you?

5. How have you experienced Jesus being Lord in your life?

## PRAYING A PASSAGE WITH GOD'S NAME

Praise Christ because he has set his affection on you. Ask him for the grace to submit every aspect of your life to his lordship. Focus on the name *Kyrios*, "Lord," as you read Deuteronomy 10:14–17.

> <sup>14</sup> Remember that the sky, the highest heaven, the earth and everything it contains belong to **Yahweh** your **Elohim**. <sup>15</sup> **Yahweh** set his heart on your ancestors and loved them. Because of this, today he chooses you, their descendants, out of all the people of the world.
>
> <sup>16</sup> So circumcise your uncircumcised hearts, and don't be impossible to deal with any longer. <sup>17</sup> There is no one like Yahweh—your one true **Elohim** and **Adonay**. He is the great, powerful, and awe-inspiring **El**. He never plays favorites and never takes a bribe.

### PRAYING THE NAME **LORD** FOR MYSELF

Look up and read: Matthew 7:21

In order to serve the Lord, you need to understand his expectations. God will give you eyes to see and a mind that understands his will. Think through the things you've done in the last day. Did you say and do things that you know were genuinely seeking the Father's will? Did you do anything that you know could keep you from him? Confess and seek the Lord in prayer.

## PROMISES FROM THE **LORD**

[8] Dear friends, don't ignore this fact: One day with the Lord is like a thousand years, and a thousand years are like one day. [9] The Lord isn't slow to do what he promised, as some people think. Rather, he is patient for your sake. He doesn't want to destroy anyone but wants all people to have an opportunity to turn to him and change the way they think and act.

[10] The day of the Lord will come like a thief. On that day heaven will pass away with a roaring sound. Everything that makes up the universe will burn and be destroyed. The earth and everything that people have done on it will be exposed.

—2 Peter 3:8-10

[10] Why do you criticize or despise other Christians? Everyone will stand in front of God to be judged. [11] Scripture says,

> "As certainly as I live, says the Lord,
> everyone will worship me,
> and everyone will praise God."

[12] All of us will have to give an account of ourselves to God.

—Romans 14:10-12

## FOR DEEPER STUDY

*Read the following passages, considering the name* **LORD** *and how its meaning relates to the context of the passage.*

Mark 10:42–45

Luke 2:8–14; 5:4–8

John 20:24–29

Philippians 2:5–11; 4:4

# FRIEND

## φίλος
### *PHILOS*

Jesus is not only Lord and Master but the greatest of all friends, who willingly proved his friendship by his death on the cross. By this costly gesture he has won the friendship of millions of men and women from every tongue and tribe and nation. When you pray to Jesus your Friend, you are praying to the one who loved you before you were loveable and the one who links you together with his many friends throughout the world.

## KEY SCRIPTURE

The greatest love you can show is to give your life for your friends.

—John 15:13

# GOD REVEALS HIS NAME IN SCRIPTURE
## JOHN 15:12–14; ROMANS 5:9–11

*Open your personal Bible translation and read the same passage. Make note where you read the word* **FRIENDS** *or* **RELATIONSHIP**

¹²Love each other as I have loved you. This is what I'm commanding you to do. ¹³The greatest love you can show is to give your life for your friends. ¹⁴You are my friends if you obey my commandments. ¹⁵I don't call you servants anymore, because a servant doesn't know what his master is doing. But I've called you friends because I've made known to you everything that I've heard from my Father.

⁹Since Christ's blood has now given us God's approval, we are even more certain that Christ will save us from God's anger. ¹⁰If the death of his Son restored our relationship with God while we were still his enemies, we are even more certain that, because of this restored relationship, the life of his Son will save us. ¹¹In addition, our Lord *Yeshua* Christ lets us continue to brag about God. After all, it is through Christ that we now have this restored relationship with God.

## UNDERSTANDING THE NAME

The Greek word **philos** (FEE-los) means "friend" or "relative." Occurring twenty-eight times in the New Testament, it is also used to describe the close relationship that exists among believers, related to each other by virtue of their faith in Jesus. This word is related to **phileo**, the most general term for "to love" in the New Testament, and to the word *philema*, which means "a kiss." In fact, the early Christians used to greet each other with a holy kiss, signifying their close relationship.

John's gospel indicates that Jesus not only called his disciples his friends but defined his own relationship with them by what was to be the greatest of all acts of friendship, in which he would lay down his life for them. Furthermore, unlike most men of his day, Jesus had both male and female friends. Luke addressed his gospel to someone named Theophilus, a proper name meaning "friend of God." The designation "friends" has survived as another name for those who belong to the religious group known as Quakers.

# CONNECTING TO THE NAME

1. What is the command that allows us to remain in Jesus' love? Why do you think that Jesus made this the key?

2. Explain in your own words how Jesus defines friendship in John 15:9–11.

3. Describe the difference between being a servant of God and becoming a true friend of Jesus.

4. Describe the best friendship you have ever had. How does it compare with the way you have experienced Jesus' friendship?

5. How can you deepen your friendship with Christ?

6. If Jesus died for us while we were still his enemies, as Romans 5:6–11 tells us, how should we regard our own enemies?

# PRAYING A PASSAGE WITH GOD'S NAME

Thank God that Jesus is not only our Lord but also our closest friend. Ask him to help you keep faith even when his friendship seems in doubt. Focus on the name *Philos*, "Friend," as you read John 11:1–6.

Lazarus, who lived in Bethany, the village where Mary and her sister Martha lived, was sick. ² (Mary was the woman who poured perfume on the Lord and wiped his feet with her hair. Her brother Lazarus was the one who was sick.)

³ So the sisters sent a messenger to tell **Yeshua**, "Lord, your close friend is sick."

⁴ When **Yeshua** heard the message, he said, "His sickness won't result in death. Instead, this sickness will bring glory to God so that the Son of God will receive glory through it."

⁵ **Yeshua** loved Martha, her sister, and Lazarus. ⁶ Yet, when **Yeshua** heard that Lazarus was sick, he stayed where he was for two more days.

## PRAYING THE NAME **FRIEND** FOR MYSELF

Look up and read: 1 Samuel 20:14–17

Have you ever loved a friend to the point of making yourself a willing sacrifice on their behalf? Jonathan made a friendship covenant with David. This is the same covenant of friendship Jesus made with us. Jesus called you his friend and claimed to be a friend to sinners, himself. How can you seek to be more of a friend like him?

_____

_____

_____

_____

# PROMISES FROM **JESUS,** OUR **FRIEND**

A friend always loves,
and a brother is born to share trouble.
—Proverbs 17:17

Perfume and incense make the heart glad,
but the sweetness of a friend is a fragrant forest.
—Proverbs 27:9

## FOR DEEPER STUDY

*Read the following passages, considering the name* **FRIEND** *and how its meaning relates to the context of the passage.*

Exodus 33:7–11

Job 29:2–6

Proverbs 18:24

Ecclesiastes 4:9–12

Matthew 11:19; 26:47–51

John 11:1–44; 21:4–7

James 2:20–24

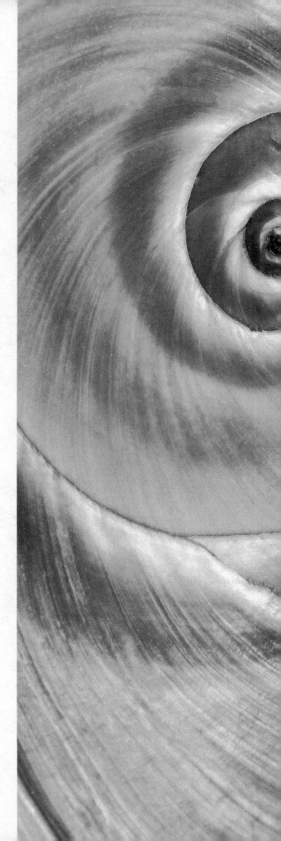

# ALPHA AND OMEGA

## ἄλφα καὶ Ὦ

### ALPHA KAI OMEGA

In the last book of the Bible, Jesus reveals himself as "the Alpha and the Omega, the First and the Last, the Beginning and the End." Present at the world's beginning, Jesus will also be present at its end, when he and his work are finally and fully revealed. When you pray to Christ as the Alpha and the Omega, you are praying to the one who is, who was, and who is to come. He is our all-sufficient Lord, who will not fail to complete the good work he has begun in us.

## KEY SCRIPTURE

I am the A and the Z [the Alpha and the Omega], the first and the last, the beginning and the end.

—Revelation 22:13

# GOD REVEALS HIS NAME IN SCRIPTURE
## ISAIAH 48:12; REVELATION 21:5–6; 22:12–13

*Open your personal Bible translation and read the same passages. Make note where you read* **FIRST AND LAST** *or* **A AND Z**

¹²Listen to me, Jacob,
　　Israel, whom I have called.
　　　　I am the one.
　　　　　　I am the first and the last.

⁵The one sitting on the throne said, "I am making everything new." He said, "Write this: 'These words are faithful and true.'" ⁶He said to me, "It has happened! I am the A and the Z [the Alpha and the Omega], the beginning and the end. I will give a drink from the fountain filled with the water of life to anyone who is thirsty. It won't cost anything.

¹²"I'm coming soon! I will bring my reward with me to pay all people based on what they have done. ¹³I am the A and the Z [the Alpha and the Omega], the first and the last, the beginning and the end.

# ἄλφα καὶ Ὦ

## UNDERSTANDING THE NAME

The title *"Alpha and Omega"* occurs only three times in the Bible, and all three are in the book of Revelation. Because Alpha and Omega are the first and last letters in the Greek alphabet, Revelation 22:13 could be translated: "I am the A and the Z, the First and the Last, the Beginning and the End." These verses in Revelation probably allude to passages in Isaiah in which God identifies himself as being both the first and the last (Isaiah 44:6; 48:12).

# CONNECTING TO THE NAME

1. Can you imagine a human being claiming to be the A to Z? Why or why not?

2. Try to relate this title, Alpha and Omega, to Jesus' role in both creation and in world history. What do you think it means?

3. How do you think this title relates to Christ's divinity?

4. What would it mean to say that Jesus is first and last in your own life?

5. Instead of looking at your life as your story, what if you viewed your life as part of God's story? What implications does this have for the way you live and the goals you have?

6. "In him we live and move and have our being" (Acts 17:28 NIV). What does this mean to you?

# PRAYING A PASSAGE WITH GOD'S NAME

Jesus as God's Word was present at the beginning when God created the world and he will be present when heaven and earth reunite on the world's last day. Praise him for his mastery over time and history. Focus on the name *Alpha Kai Omega*, the "Alpha and the Omega," as you read Colossians 1:15–20.

> He is the image of the invisible God,
>> the firstborn of all creation.
> [16] He created all things in heaven and on earth,
>> visible and invisible.
>>> Whether they are kings or lords,
>>>> rulers or powers—
>>>>> everything has been created through him
>>>>> and for him.
> [17] He existed before everything
>> and holds everything together.
> [18] He is also the head of the church, which is his body.
>> He is the beginning,
>>> the first to come back to life
>>>> so that he would have first place in everything.

[19] God was pleased to have all of himself live in Christ. [20] God was also pleased to bring everything on earth and in heaven back to himself through Christ. He did this by making peace through Christ's blood sacrificed on the cross.

## PRAYING THE NAME
## THE **ALPHA AND** THE **OMEGA** FOR MYSELF

Look up and read: Revelation 1:7–8

Praise Christ for not only being the **Alpha and the Omega**, which are the first and last letters of the Greek alphabet, but also for being all the letters in between. He is the Word of God, who perfectly communicates God to us.

_____

_____

_____

# PROMISES FROM THE
# ALPHA AND THE OMEGA

³I thank my God for all the memories I have of you. ⁴Every time I pray for all of you, I do it with joy. ⁵I can do this because of the partnership we've had with you in the Good News from the first day you believed until now. ⁶I'm convinced that God, who began this good work in you, will carry it through to completion on the day of Christ *Yeshua*.

—Philippians 1:3-6

⁸"To the messenger of the church in Smyrna, write:

The first and the last, who was dead and became alive, says: ⁹I know how you are suffering, how poor you are—but you are rich. I also know that those who claim to be Jews slander you. They are the synagogue of Satan. ¹⁰Don't be afraid of what you are going to suffer. The devil is going to throw some of you into prison so that you may be tested. Your suffering will go on for ten days. Be faithful until death, and I will give you the crown of life.

¹¹Let the person who has ears listen to what the Spirit says to the churches. Everyone who wins the victory will never be hurt by the second death.

—Revelation 2:8-11

## FOR DEEPER STUDY

*Read the following passages, considering the name the* **ALPHA AND OMEGA** *and how its meaning relates to the context of the passage.*

John 1:1–3; 8:54–58

Hebrews 13:8

Revelation 1:7–8, 12–13, 17–18

# JESUS THE SAVIOR

## Ἰησοῦς σωτήρ
### IESOUS SOTER

Just as *Yahweh* is God's personal name revealed in the Old Testament, Jesus is the personal name of the one we call Redeemer, Lord, and Christ. His name is intimately linked to the God of the Hebrew Scriptures because it means "Yahweh Is Salvation." Indeed, Jesus is *Yahweh* come to earth. If you have ever pictured God as a distant, wrathful Being, you will have to reconsider that portrait in light of Jesus Christ, who is God bending toward us, God becoming one of us, God reaching out in mercy, God humbling himself, God nailed to a cross, God rising up from the grave to show us the way home. Jesus, name above all names, beautiful Savior, glorious Lord!

## KEY SCRIPTURE

The angel said to him, "Joseph, descendant of David, don't be afraid to take Mary as your wife. She is pregnant by the Holy Spirit. She will give birth to a son, and you will name him **Yeshua** [He Saves], because he will save his people from their sins."

—Matthew 1:20–21

# GOD REVEALS HIS NAME IN SCRIPTURE
## MATTHEW 1:18–25

*Open your personal Bible translation and read the same passage. Make note where you read the word* **SAVE**.

[18] The birth of **Yeshua** Christ took place in this way. His mother Mary had been promised to Joseph in marriage. But before they were married, Mary realized that she was pregnant by the Holy Spirit. [19] Her husband Joseph was an honorable man and did not want to disgrace her publicly. So he decided to break the marriage agreement with her secretly.

[20] Joseph had this in mind when an angel of the Lord appeared to him in a dream. The angel said to him, "Joseph, descendant of David, don't be afraid to take Mary as your wife. She is pregnant by the Holy Spirit. [21] She will give birth to a son, and you will name him **Yeshua** [He Saves], because he will save his people from their sins." [22] All this happened so that what the Lord had spoken through the prophet came true: [23] "The virgin will become pregnant and give birth to a son, and they will name him Immanuel," which means "God is with us."

[24] When Joseph woke up, he did what the angel of the Lord had commanded him to do. He took Mary to be his wife. [25] He did not have marital relations with her before she gave birth to a son. Joseph named the child **Yeshua**.

# Ἰησοῦς σωτήρ

## UNDERSTANDING THE NAME

"Jesus" was a common name in first-century Palestine, and it has been found on various grave markers and tombs in and around Jerusalem. To distinguish him from others, Jesus is sometimes referred to in the Gospels as Jesus of Nazareth, Jesus the son of Joseph, or Jesus the Nazarene. Later on, he is referred to as "Jesus Christ," as though Christ is his surname.

The name "Jesus" (in English ) or *Iesous* (in Greek) is the equivalent of the Hebrew *"Yeshua,"* itself a contraction of the Hebrew name *"Yehoshua,"* translated "Joshua" in English Bibles. The name Joshua is the oldest name containing *Yahweh*, the covenant name of God, a name so sacred it was considered too holy to pronounce. Both "Jesus" and "Joshua" mean *"Yahweh* Is Help" or *"Yahweh* Is Salvation." *Yeshua* is also related to the word *yeshu'ah*, which means "salvation."

*"Soter"* is the Greek word translated "Savior." Its Hebrew equivalent is *Moshia*. In Greek, "Jesus the Savior" is rendered *Iesous Soter* (yay-SOUS so-TAIR). Through the centuries, the church has affirmed the belief of the earliest followers of Jesus that "Salvation is found in no one else, for there is no other name given under heaven by which we must be saved" (Acts 4:12 NIV).

## CONNECTING TO THE NAME

1. What comes to mind when you hear the name "Jesus"?

2. Though "Jesus" was a common name in first-century Palestine, God sent an angel to announce the name to Joseph. Comment on the significance of this.

3. Describe what Joseph might have thought and felt when the angel said that this baby would save God's people from their sin.

4. In what circumstances in your life do you need to proclaim the powerful, saving name of Jesus?

5. Why do you think Jesus' name is linked to the name of *Yahweh*, the covenant name of God in the Hebrew Scriptures?

6. Describe what salvation means to you.

## PRAYING A PASSAGE WITH GOD'S NAME

Thank God that his promise of salvation is embedded in his Son's name. Confess any complacency toward those who are lost. Ask Jesus to assign your heart with his purposes. Focus on the name *Iesous Soter*, "Jesus the Savior," as you read Luke 19:8–10.

> [8] Later, at dinner, Zacchaeus stood up and said to the Lord, "Lord, I'll give half of my property to the poor. I'll pay four times as much as I owe to those I have cheated in any way."
>
> [9] Then **Yeshua** said to Zacchaeus, "You and your family have been saved today. You've shown that you, too, are one of Abraham's descendants. Indeed the Son of Man has come to seek and to save people who are lost."

*PRAYING THE NAME OF* **JESUS THE SAVIOR** *FOR MYSELF*

Look up and read: Luke 15:1–7

When you are lost, **Jesus the Savior** longs to find you. He will stop at nothing, except your own adamant refusal, to bring you back to him. Think about a time when you were lost, and praise Jesus for saving you.

_____

_____

_____

_____

## PROMISES FROM **JESUS THE SAVIOR**

[38] Peter answered them, "All of you must turn to God and change the way you think and act, and each of you must be baptized in the name of **Yeshua** Christ so that your sins will be forgiven. Then you will receive the Holy Spirit as a gift. [39] This promise belongs to you and to your children and to everyone who is far away. It belongs to everyone who worships the Lord our God."

—Acts 2:38-39

[30] **Yeshua** performed many other miracles that his disciples saw. Those miracles are not written in this book. [31] But these miracles have been written so that you will believe that **Yeshua** is the Messiah, the Son of God, and so that you will have life by believing in him.

—John 20:30-31

*FOR DEEPER STUDY*

*Read the following passages, considering the name* **JESUS THE SAVIOR** *and how its meaning relates to the context of the passage.*

Luke 2:11–14    John 3:16    Acts 4:1–12    Romans 5:9–11    Titus 3:3–8

# BRIDE-GROOM, HUSBAND

## νυμφίος NYMPHIOS
## ἀνήρ ANER

God is not content to be known merely as Creator, Lord, or even Father. Incredibly he reveals himself also as Bridegroom or Husband. The Hebrew Scriptures contain numerous allusions to Yahweh as Israel's divine Husband, and the New Testament presents Christ as the church's Bridegroom. He is the Holy One who did not cling to his divinity, but left his Father's house to dwell among us, calling us to become one with him in the most intimate way possible. To all of us, male and female, Christ offers himself as our Provider and Protector, the one who has forever pledged himself in faithfulness and love.

## KEY SCRIPTURE

Then the angel said to me, "Write this: 'Blessed are those who are invited to the lamb's wedding banquet.'"

—Revelation 19:9

# GOD REVEALS HIS NAME IN SCRIPTURE
### ISAIAH 54:5–7; REVELATION 19:6–9

*Open your personal Bible translation and read the same passages.*
*Make note where you read the word* **HUSBAND**, **BRIDE**, *or* **WEDDING**.

Your husband is your maker.
His name is ***Yahweh Tsebaoth***.
Your ***Go'el*** is ***Qedosh Yisrael***.
He is called the ***Elohim*** of the whole earth.
"***Yahweh*** has called you as if you were
a wife who was abandoned and in grief,
a wife who married young and was rejected," says your ***Elohim***.
"I abandoned you for one brief moment,
but I will bring you back with unlimited compassion.

I heard what sounded like the noise from a large crowd, like the noise of raging waters, like the noise of loud thunder, saying,

"Hallelujah! The Lord our God, the Almighty, has become king.
Let us rejoice, be happy, and give him glory
because it's time for the marriage of the lamb.
His bride has made herself ready. She has been
given the privilege of wearing
dazzling, pure linen."

This fine linen represents the things that God's holy people do that have his approval.

Then the angel said to me, "Write this: 'Blessed are those who are invited to the lamb's wedding banquet.'" He also told me, "These are the true words of God."

# νυμφίος    ἀνήρ

## UNDERSTANDING THE NAME

Marriage in Israel was generally considered sacred, the only acceptable state of life for men and women. Despite polygamous practices, whereby a man could marry more than one wife, monogamy was the accepted pattern throughout most of biblical history, especially after the patriarchal period.

Most marriages were arranged by parents. The minimum age for girls was twelve and for boys was thirteen. The period of engagement or betrothal usually lasted a year and was considered so binding that a man who had intimate relations with a virgin betrothed to another man would be stoned. For the year following the marriage, the husband was exempt from military service. This practice prevented the bride from becoming a widow in her first year of marriage and it also allowed the man to devote himself more fully to his wife at the start of their marriage. Though the marriage ceremony itself was brief, the celebration surrounding it could be elaborate, consisting of seven and sometimes fourteen days of feasting and celebrating. During the festivities, dating from the time of Solomon, both bride and groom were crowned as king and queen and their virtues were extolled in song and poetry.

The Hebrew Scriptures did not hesitate to describe the relationship between God and his people in the most intimate of terms: *Yahweh* was the husband of Israel, his not-so-faithful wife. By referring to himself as the bridegroom, Jesus was clearly linking himself with *Yahweh*. New Testament writers presented the church as the bride of Christ. *Nymphios* (num-FEE-os) is the Greek word for "bridegroom" or "young husband" while *aner* (an-AIR) can be translated "man" or "husband."

When the disciples of John the Baptist asked Jesus why his disciples did not fast, Jesus replied that it was not possible for the guests of the bridegroom to mourn as long as he was with them (Matthew 9:14–15). John the Baptist used similar imagery when he referred to himself as the "friend who attends the bridegroom"—that is, the best man (John 3:29).

# CONNECTING TO THE NAME

1. What does the passage from Isaiah reveal about God's character?

2. What does it reveal about the nature of his relationship with his chosen people?

3. How does the passage from Revelation compare and contrast with the passage from Isaiah?

4. Describe why the Bible is best understood not as a rule book or a compendium of wisdom but as a love story.

5. How have you experienced God protecting and providing for you as a loving husband?

6. In what ways might you spurn the love of Jesus? What pulls you away from him? What tempts you to look elsewhere for help, hope, and fulfillment?

# PRAYING A PASSAGE WITH GOD'S NAME

Rejoice because of God's ultimate plans to dwell intimately with his people. Ask him to help you and the church to prepare for the day of his coming. Focus on the name *Nymphios*, or "Bridegroom," as you read Revelation 21:1–3.

I saw a new heaven and a new earth, because the first heaven and earth had disappeared, and the sea was gone. ² Then I saw the holy city, New Jerusalem, coming down from God out of heaven, dressed like a bride ready for her husband. ³ I heard a loud voice from the throne say, "God lives with humans! God will make his home with them, and they will be his people. God himself will be with them and be their God.

### *PRAYING THE NAME* **BRIDEGROOM** *OR* **HUSBAND** *FOR MYSELF*

Look up and read: Matthew 25:1–13

Jesus tells a parable about 10 virgins who went out to meet the Bridegroom before the wedding feast. Five were prepared, and five were totally unprepared. Ask Jesus what you need to do to prepare wisely for his coming.

# PROMISES FROM YOUR **BRIDEGROOM**

As a young man marries a woman,
   so your sons will marry you.
As a bridegroom rejoices over his bride,
   so your *Elohim* will rejoice over you.
—Isaiah 62:5

"Israel, I will make you my wife forever.
   I will be honest and faithful to you.
   I will show you my love and compassion.
[20] I will be true to you, my wife.
   Then you will know *Yahweh*.
   —Hosea 2:19–20

## FOR DEEPER STUDY

*Read the following passages, considering the name* **BRIDEGROOM** *or* **HUSBAND** *and how its meaning relates to the context of the passage.*

Isaiah 61:10–62:5

Jeremiah 3:14–17, 20

Hosea 2:13–3:1

Matthew 22:1–14

John 14:1–3

Romans 7:1–6

Revelation 21:9–27; 22:1–17

# SON OF DAVID

## υἱὸς Δαυίδ

### UIOS DAUID

David was Israel's greatest king, a man whom the Bible describes as having the very heart of God. So it may not be surprising that the New Testament both begins and ends with references to Jesus as the Son or Offspring of David. He is the one who fulfilled the promise of a coming King so beloved by God that his throne will endure forever. Like David, Jesus was born in Bethlehem (the city of David). And like David, who established his kingdom by overcoming Israel's enemies and uniting God's people, Jesus established his kingdom by defeating the principalities and powers, making a way for us to become part of it as we confess our faith in him. When you pray to Jesus as the Son of David, you are praying to the long-awaited King, human by virtue of his descent from David and divine by virtue of being God's only Son.

## KEY SCRIPTURE

He will be a great man
and will be called the Son of the Most High.
The Lord God will give him
the throne of his ancestor David.
Your son will be king of Jacob's people forever,
and his kingdom will never end."
—Luke 1:32–33

# CHRIST REVEALS HIS NAME IN SCRIPTURE
## 1 CHRONICLES 17:7–14; LUKE 1:26–33

*Open your personal Bible translation and read the same passages. Make note where you read the name* **DAVID**.

"Now this is what you will say to my servant David: 'This is what **Yahweh Tsebaoth** says: I took you from the pasture where you followed sheep so that you could be the leader of my people Israel. I was with you wherever you went, and I destroyed all your enemies in front of you. I will make your name like the names of the greatest people on earth. I will make a place for my people Israel and plant them there. They will live in their own place and not be troubled anymore. The wicked will no longer frighten them as they used to do ever since I appointed judges to rule my people Israel. I will crush all your enemies. I even tell you that I, **Yahweh**, will build a house for you.

"'When the time comes for you to go and be with your ancestors, I will send one of your descendants. He will be one of your sons. I will establish his kingdom. He will build a house for me, and I will establish his throne forever. I will be his **Ab**, and he will be my Son. And I will never stop showing him my love as I did to your predecessor. I will place him in my royal house forever, and his throne will be established forever.'"

Six months after Elizabeth had become pregnant, God sent the angel Gabriel to Nazareth, a city in Galilee. [27] The angel went to a virgin promised in marriage to a descendant of David named Joseph. The virgin's name was Mary.

When the angel entered her home, he greeted her and said, "You are favored by the Lord! The Lord is with you."

She was startled by what the angel said and tried to figure out what this greeting meant.

The angel told her,

> "Don't be afraid, Mary. You have found favor with God.
> You will become pregnant, give birth to a son,
>     and name him **Yeshua**.
> He will be a great man
>     and will be called the Son of the Most High.
>     The Lord God will give him
>     the throne of his ancestor David.
> Your son will be king of Jacob's people forever,
>     and his kingdom will never end."

# υἱὸς Δαυίδ

## UNDERSTANDING THE NAME

The New Testament tells a story that cannot be adequately understood without reference to the Old Testament. Though composed of many books written at different times by different authors, much of the Bible is a continuing narrative that tells the story of salvation in ever-deepening detail. One of the ways it does this is by encapsulating the story or part of the story in the life of a particular person in the Bible whose shadow is then cast forward across the remaining pages of the Bible.

David is certainly one of these characters, for in many ways his life prefigures the life of Christ. Like Christ, David conquered against incredible odds. Like Christ, he was beloved of God. And like Christ, he was a warrior king who defeated God's enemies. David began as a shepherd boy signifying Jesus' coming role as the good Shepherd who would lay down his life for his sheep.

The Gospels refer to Jesus as the "Son of David" or *Huios Dauid* (hui-OS da-WEED) fifteen times, nine of these in Matthew. Many of the Jews at the time of Jesus believed that the Messiah would be a direct descendant of the great King David, whom God described "as a man after my own heart." More than once in the Gospels, people in need of healing cried out to Jesus as the "Son of David," thus confessing their faith in him as the long-awaited Messiah. The New Testament also refers to Jesus as the "Root and Offspring of David," the "descendant" or "seed" of David, and the one who

# υἱὸς Δαυίδ

holds the "key of David." Along with acknowledging Jesus as the rightful heir to David's throne, the title "Son of David" also locates Jesus within a human genealogy, that of Abraham and David.

## CONNECTING TO THE NAME

1. Do you think the prophecy recounted in 1 Chronicles was fulfilled in the life of David's son Solomon? Why or why not? (See 1 Kings 11:1–13.)

2. Compare the lives of Jesus and David. What similarities do you see? What differences?

3. Consider how different life might be if you lived under a corrupt or incompetent government. Now think of how different life might be if you lived in a country that was perfectly governed, ruled by a leader who was all-powerful, all-wise, and all-loving. Describe the differences.

4. What difficulties do you face? What would happen if you saw every difficulty as an opportunity for Jesus, as the Son of David, to extend his rule over you?

5. What areas of your life are not yet fully under Christ's rule? What specific things could you do right now to change that?

6. What do you think it means to be a man or woman "after God's own heart"? How is God's heart already manifested in you?

# PRAYING A PASSAGE WITH GOD'S NAME

Ask Jesus, the Son of David, to extend his rule over you, vanquishing the sins you feel most powerless against. Focus on the name *Huios Dauid*, "Son of David," as you read Mark 12:35–37.

> [35] While **Yeshua** was teaching in the temple courtyard, he asked, "How can the experts in Moses' Teachings say that the Messiah is David's son? [36] David, guided by the Holy Spirit, said,
>
> > 'The Lord said to my Lord:
> > > "Take the highest position in heaven
> > > > until I put your enemies under your control." '
> > [37] David calls him Lord. So how can he be his son?"

### PRAYING THE NAME SON OF DAVID FOR MYSELF

Look up and read: 2 Timothy 2:8–10

One of the reasons that we are reminded that Jesus is the Son of David and of a real human lineage is to remind us that Jesus redeems all history. Think of the beauty and the brokenness in your own family history, and praise Jesus for the ways that he has redeemed the people who came before you.

_____

_____

_____

_____

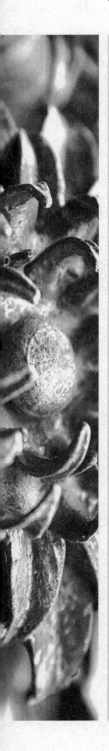

# PROMISES FROM THE **SON OF DAVID**

Then a shoot will come out from the stump of Jesse,
    and a branch from its roots will bear fruit.
    ² The **Ruach\* Yahweh** will rest on him—
    the **Ruach** of wisdom and understanding,
    the **Ruach** of advice and power,
    the **Ruach** of knowledge and fear of **Yahweh**.
³ He will gladly bear the fear of **Yahweh**.
    He will not judge by what his eyes see
    or decide by what his ears hear.
⁴ He will judge the poor justly.
    He will make fair decisions for the humble people on
        earth.
    He will strike the earth with a rod from his mouth.
    He will kill the wicked with the breath from his lips.

                *\* Ruach is translated "Spirit."*

—Isaiah 11:1-4


A child will be born for us.
    A son will be given to us.
    The government will rest on his shoulders.
    He will be named:
        Wonderful Counselor,
        Mighty God,
        Everlasting Father,
        **Sar Shalom**.
⁷ His government and peace will have unlimited growth.
    He will establish David's throne and kingdom.
    He will uphold it with justice and righteousness now and
        forever.
    **Yahweh Tsebaoth** is determined to do this!
—Isaiah 9:6-7

## FOR DEEPER STUDY

*Read the following passages, considering the name* **SON OF DAVID** *and how its meaning relates to the context of the passage.*

Matthew 1:1–2:12

Acts 13:21–39

Revelation 5:1–5; 22:16

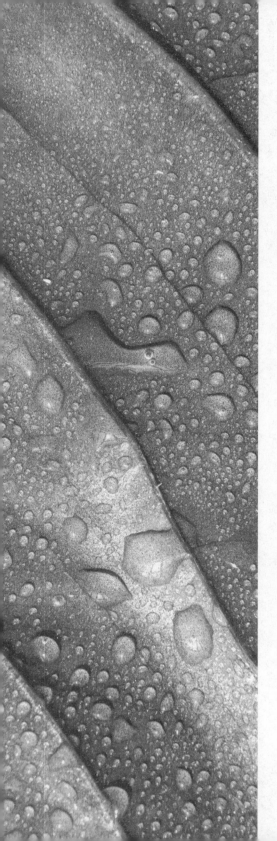

# PRIEST, PROPHET

ἱερεύς *HIEREUS*
προφήτης *PROPHETES*

Jesus is both Priest—the one who faithfully bears us into God's presence by virtue of his self-sacrifice—and Prophet—the one who perfectly communicates God's Word to us. We are called to listen to him, to trust in his work, and to take our places as part of a kingdom of priests, who in Christ Jesus offer ourselves on behalf of others. As you pray to Jesus as both Priest and Prophet, ask him to help you understand the deep meaning of these titles so that you can live out their truths in your life.

## KEY SCRIPTURES

We need to hold on to our declaration of faith: We have a superior chief priest who has gone through the heavens. That person is **Yeshua**, the Son of God.

—Hebrews 4:14

In the past God spoke to our ancestors at many different times and in many different ways through the prophets. In these last days he has spoken to us through his Son. God made his Son responsible for everything.

—Hebrews 1:1–2a

# CHRIST REVEALS HIS NAME IN SCRIPTURE
## HEBREWS 4:14–16; DEUTERONOMY 18:15–18

*Open your personal Bible translation and read the same passages. Make note where you read the name* **PRIEST** *or* **PROPHET**.

We need to hold on to our declaration of faith: We have a superior chief priest who has gone through the heavens. That person is **Yeshua**, the Son of God. We have a chief priest who is able to sympathize with our weaknesses. He was tempted in every way that we are, but he didn't sin. So we can go confidently to the throne of God's kindness to receive mercy and find kindness, which will help us at the right time.

**Yahweh** your **Elohim** will send you a prophet, an Israelite like me. You must listen to him. This is what you asked **Yahweh** your **Elohim** to give you on the day of the assembly at Mount Horeb. You said, "We never want to hear the voice of **Yahweh** our **Elohim** or see this raging fire again. If we do, we'll die!"

**Yahweh** told me, "What they've said is good. So I will send them a prophet, an Israelite like you. I will put my words in his mouth. He will tell them everything I command him.

# προφήτης

## UNDERSTANDING THE NAME

Prophet, priest, and king—these were the three major offices in Israel, titles also ascribed to Jesus. While the king governed as God's representative on earth, the priest's role was to represent the people to God by offering sacrifices, prayers, and praise on their behalf. Unlike kings and priests, which were normally hereditary offices held only by males, prophets had to be commissioned by God, and they could be either male or female.

The role of the priest was to bring the people before God. Moses' brother, Aaron, was the first Israelite priest. Thereafter priests were drawn from among his descendants, and they were given charge of worship, which eventually became centralized in the Jerusalem temple. Unlike worship in many churches today, Jewish worship primarily consisted not in singing songs and listening to sermons but in offering sacrifices as prescribed by the Mosaic law. The priest's role was to offer sacrifices for his own sins and for the sins of the people. The animals killed for this purpose served as a continual reminder to both priests and people that the penalty for sin is death.

The priesthood consisted of three groups: the high priest, ordinary priests, and Levites. The Levites occupied the lowest rung of the ladder, taking care of the temple service. The priests, who alone could offer sacrifices, were next. At the pinnacle stood the high priest, the only one authorized to enter the Most Holy Place on the Day of Atonement. On his ephod (a garment attached to the breast piece) were stones that bore the names of the twelve tribes of Israel, a physical reminder that the high priest was bearing the people into God's presence.

The New Testament identifies Jesus as a priest according to the order of Melchizedek (Melchizedek, a priest who was a contemporary of Abraham, predated the Levites). This was a way of indicating that his priesthood was both different from and superior to that of the Levitical priesthood. Though most priests in Jerusalem at the time of Jesus rejected him, the book of Hebrews, emphasizing Jesus' role as High Priest, may have been aimed primarily at priests who became believers after the resurrection. The Greek word for "priest" is *hierus* (hee-eh-REUS).

While the primary role of the priest was to speak to God on behalf of the people, the prophet's primary responsibility was to speak to the people on behalf of God.

# ἱερεύς

The great prophets of the Hebrew Scriptures included Moses, Isaiah, Jeremiah, Elijah, and Elisha. While prophets sometimes predicted future events, more often they called people to faithfulness.

Jesus acknowledged that his cousin, John, was a prophet—and more than a prophet because he prophesied most clearly about the Messiah. Though the common people acclaimed Jesus as a prophet and though he seemed comfortable with this title, most of the priests rejected this title for Jesus. In a Jewish context, Jesus' baptism in the Jordan, when the Spirit descended on him, would have been understood as a time in which he was commissioned by God as a prophet. But unlike the prophets who preceded him, Jesus would be the one Prophet who not only perfectly revealed God's Word but who perfectly revealed God himself.

The New Testament identifies several people besides John the Baptist as prophets or as people who prophesied at one time or another. These included John's father, Zechariah; Elizabeth; Simeon; Anna; the high priest Caiphas; Agabus; and Barnabas. The New Testament also indicates that there were prophets in the early church and that prophecy was considered one of the spiritual gifts. The Greek word *prophetes* (pro-PHAY-tays) is found 144 times in the New Testament, which, in proportion to its length, contains as many references to prophets and prophecies as do the Hebrew Scriptures.

## CONNECTING TO THE NAME

1. Why do you think it is important that Jesus, as High Priest, is able to sympathize with our weakness?

2. What about Jesus made him capable of sympathizing with us?

3. The role of a priest is to bring people before God and to speak to God on their behalf. How has Jesus performed this role in your life?

4. Why do you think Jesus was more effective than the priests of the Old Testament?

5. A prophet's job is to speak to the people on behalf of God. How has Jesus fulfilled this role in your life?

## PRAYING A PASSAGE WITH GOD'S NAME

Praise God for making Jesus his final perfect communication to his people. Thank Jesus for holding everything together and showing us who God is. Focus on the names *Hiereus*, "Priest," and *Prophetes*, "Prophet," as you read Hebrews 1:1–3.

> In the past God spoke to our ancestors at many different times and in many different ways through the prophets. [2] In these last days he has spoken to us through his Son. God made his Son responsible for everything. His Son is the one through whom God made the universe. [3] His Son is the reflection of God's glory and the exact likeness of God's being. He holds everything together through his powerful words. After he had cleansed people from their sins, he received the highest position, the one next to the Father in heaven.

PRAYING THE NAMES
**PRIEST** AND **PROPHET** FOR MYSELF

Look up and read: 1 Peter 2:9–10

Jesus is the great high priest, and you are a part of a royal priesthood. How do you react to this title? Are you able to receive it with God's grace, or do you feel yourself rejecting that role or merely relegating it to a metaphor?

_____

_____

_____

_____

# PROMISES FROM JESUS, OUR **PRIEST** AND **PROPHET**

"Don't be troubled. Believe in God, and believe in me. ²My Father's house has many rooms. If that were not true, would I have told you that I'm going to prepare a place for you? ³If I go to prepare a place for you, I will come again. Then I will bring you into my presence so that you will be where I am.

—John 14:1–3

What can we say about all of this? If God is for us, who can be against us? ³²God didn't spare his own Son but handed him over to death for all of us. So he will also give us everything along with him. ³³Who will accuse those whom God has chosen? God has approved of them. ³⁴Who will condemn them? Christ has died, and more importantly, he was brought back to life. Christ has the highest position in heaven. Christ also intercedes for us.

—Romans 8:31–34

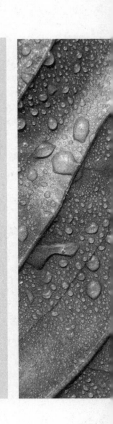

## FOR DEEPER STUDY

*Read the following passages, considering the names* **PRIEST** *and* **PROPHET** *and how their meanings relate to the context of the passage.*

Leviticus 16

Matthew 13:54–58; 17:1–5

Luke 24:17–27

Acts 2:14–18

1 Corinthians 14:1–3

1 Timothy 2:5

Hebrews 2:14–18; 5:4–6; 7:23–9:15; 10:19–23

1 Peter 2:4–5

# SON OF GOD, SON OF MAN

## υἱὸς τοῦ θεοῦ, υἱὸς
### HUIOS TOU THEOU

## τοῦ ἀνθρώπου
### HUIOS TOU ANTHROPOU

Like the Father and the Holy Spirit, Jesus is God. He always was, always is, and always will be. But unlike the Father and the Spirit, Jesus is also a human being. Though charged with blasphemy and crucified for claiming to be one with the Father, Jesus' resurrection validates his claim to be God's Son in a unique way. When we confess our belief that Jesus is the Son of God, we share in the love the Father has for the Son, becoming adopted children of God.

Though Jesus was the Son of God, he was also the Son of Man, a title that emphasizes both his lowliness and his eventual dominion. Near the end of his life, when the high priest asked him whether he was the Son of God, Jesus no longer avoided the title but said that he would one day "see the Son of Man sitting at the right hand of the Mighty One and coming on the clouds of heaven" (Matthew 26:64). When you pray to Jesus as Son of God and Son of Man, you are praying to the One who is your Brother and your Lord.

## KEY SCRIPTURE

He asked them, "But who do you say I am?"

Simon Peter answered, "You are the Messiah, the Son of the living God!"

*Yeshua* replied, "Simon, son of Jonah, you are blessed! No human revealed this to you, but my Father in heaven revealed it to you.

—Matthew 16:15–17

# CHRIST REVEALS HIS NAME IN SCRIPTURE
## DANIEL 7:13–14; MATTHEW 16:13–21

*Open your personal Bible translation and read the same passages. Make note where the* **SON OF GOD** *or the* **SON OF MAN** *is used as God's name.*

In my visions during the night, I saw among the clouds in heaven someone like the *Bar-Enash*. He came to the Ancient One, who has lived for endless years, and was presented to him. He was given power, honor, and a kingdom. People from every province, nation, and language were to serve him. His power is an eternal power that will not be taken away. His kingdom will never be destroyed.

When *Yeshua* came to the region of Caesarea Philippi, he asked his disciples, "Who do people say the Son of Man is?"

They answered, "Some say you are John the Baptizer, others Elijah, still others Jeremiah or one of the prophets."

He asked them, "But who do you say I am?"

Simon Peter answered, "You are the Messiah, the Son of the living God!"

*Yeshua* replied, "Simon, son of Jonah, you are blessed! No human revealed this to you, but my Father in heaven revealed it to you. You are Peter, and I can guarantee that on this rock I will build my church. And the gates of hell will not overpower it. I will give you the keys of the kingdom of heaven. Whatever you imprison, God will imprison. And whatever you set free, God will set free."

Then he strictly ordered the disciples not to tell anyone that he was the Messiah.

From that time on *Yeshua* began to inform his disciples that he had to go to Jerusalem. There he would have to suffer a lot because of the leaders, the chief priests, and the experts in Moses' Teachings. He would be killed, but on the third day he would be brought back to life.

# υἱὸς τοῦ θεοῦ, υἱὸς

## UNDERSTANDING THE NAME

Though the phrase "sons of God" was occasionally used in the Hebrew Scriptures, the Greek phrase "Son of God," *Huios tou Theou* (hui-OS tou the-OU) belongs to Jesus in a unique way. Jesus himself indicates that he and the Father are one. He is the only man who could bear the title without dishonoring the Father.

But Jesus is God's Son not in the sense that most Westerners think of sonship, as though the Father preexisted him. Instead, Jesus is God's Son in the sense that he shares his nature and represents his intentions. He is fully divine and therefore perfectly capable of representing the Father on earth. Twice in the Gospels—at Jesus' baptism and at the transfiguration—a voice from heaven announced: "This is my Son, whom I love."

During Jesus' earthly ministry, even the demons recognized Christ as the "Son of God." However, it was this politically charged title that led to Jesus' death, which may be why he avoided it until the end of his life. Recognizing this as a primary title of Christ, the early church baptized those who confessed Jesus Christ as the Son of God. These early believers understood, as we do, that our relationship with Christ enables us to become adopted children of the Father.

Though Jesus was the Son of God, his favorite title for himself was the "Son of Man," *Huios tou Anthropou* (hui-OS tou an-THROW- pou). It's a somewhat enigmatic title.

# τοῦ ἀνθρώπου

But certainly one meaning of it is that Jesus is the perfect human being. He shows us through his life on earth what men and women were intended by God to be before we fell prey to sin. But the title also has messianic connotations and is closely connected with Jesus' second coming. The passage from Daniel 7:13–14 is speaking of a powerful messianic king.

Together the titles Son of Man and Son of God express the incredible mystery of the incarnation—that the second person of the Trinity came down from heaven to become one of us so that we could be one with him. When Jesus rose from the dead, he ascended into heaven, not just as God but also as a man. C. S. Lewis remarked on this truth: "I seldom meet any strong or exultant sense of the continued, never-to-be-abandoned, Humanity of Christ in glory, in eternity. We stress the Humanity too exclusively at Christmas, and the Deity too exclusively after the Resurrection; almost as if Christ once became a man and then presently reverted to being simply God. We think of the Resurrection and Ascension (rightly) as great acts of God; less often as the triumph of Man."

## CONNECTING TO THE NAME

1. How did Jesus fulfill Daniel's vision of "one like *Bar-Erash*, a son of man"?

2. What do you think it means to say that Jesus is the Son of God?

3. Why do you think Jesus cautioned his disciples against telling anyone that he was the Messiah?

4. Describe your image of the ideal father. How does this compare with your image of who God is?

5. Describe your image of the ideal son or daughter. How does this compare with your image of yourself in relationship to God?

6. How does Jesus as the ideal human being reflect your understanding of God's purpose for all human beings?

## PRAYING A PASSAGE WITH GOD'S NAME

Thank God for revealing Jesus as his Son to you. Ask him to deepen your own understanding of being his son or daughter. Focus on the name *Huios Tou Theou,* "Son of God" and *Huios Tou Anthropou,* "Son of Man," as you read Matthew 27:50–54.

[50] Then **Yeshua** loudly cried out once again and gave up his life.

[51] Suddenly, the curtain in the temple was split in two from top to bottom. The earth shook, and the rocks were split open. [52] The tombs were opened, and the bodies of many holy people who had died came back to life. [53] They came out of the tombs after he had come back to life, and they went into the holy city where they appeared to many people.

[54] An army officer and those watching **Yeshua** with him saw the earthquake and the other things happening. They were terrified and said, "Certainly, this was the Son of God!"

## *PRAYING THE NAMES* **SON OF GOD** *AND* **SON OF MAN** *FOR MYSELF*

Look up and read: Matthew 16:13–16

Unbelievers are blinded to Jesus' true identity. Pray and ask God to open the eyes of the blind. Ask him to make you into a "little Christ" so that others may know him.

_____

_____

_____

_____

_____

# PROMISES FROM THE **SON OF GOD** AND **SON OF MAN**

[4] But when the right time came, God sent his Son into the world. A woman gave birth to him, and he came under the control of the laws given to Moses. [5] God sent him to pay for the freedom of those who were controlled by these laws so that we would be adopted as his children. [6] Because you are God's children, God has sent the Spirit of his Son into us to call out, "Abba! Father!" [7] So you are no longer slaves but God's children. Since you are God's children, God has also made you heirs.

—Galatians 4:4-7

[27] The Son of Man will come with his angels in his Father's glory. Then he will pay back each person based on what that person has done.

—Matthew 16:27

## FOR DEEPER STUDY

*Read the following passages, considering the names* **SON OF GOD** *and* **SON OF MAN** *and how their meanings relate to the context of the passage.*

Matthew 12:38–42; 20:20–28; 25:31–33; 26:63–66

Mark 9:2–7

John 3:16–17; 14:12–14

Romans 8:14–17, 28–30

2 Corinthians 6:18

Hebrews 1:1–5

1 John 4:9–12

Revelation 1:12–18

# GOOD SHEPHERD

## ποιμὴν καλός
### POIMEN KALOS

One of the most tender images of Jesus is one he supplied when referring to himself as the Good Shepherd. This name reminds us of our own vulnerability and of Jesus' watchful, protecting care. It evokes a sense of belonging, intimacy, and trust, revealing the Good Shepherd as the one who lays down his life for his sheep. When you pray to the Good Shepherd, you are admitting your need for his care and your confidence in his ability to watch over and protect you.

## KEY SCRIPTURE

"I am the good shepherd. The good shepherd gives his life for the sheep."

—John 10:11

# CHRIST REVEALS HIS NAME IN SCRIPTURE
## JOHN 10:1-18

*Open your personal Bible translation and read the same passage. Make note where you read the name* **SHEPHERD**.

"I can guarantee this truth: The person who doesn't enter the sheep pen through the gate but climbs in somewhere else is a thief or a robber. But the one who enters through the gate is the shepherd. The gatekeeper opens the gate for him, and the sheep respond to his voice. He calls his sheep by name and leads them out of the pen. After he has brought out all his sheep, he walks ahead of them. The sheep follow him because they recognize his voice. They won't follow a stranger. Instead, they will run away from a stranger because they don't recognize his voice." **Yeshua** used this illustration as he talked to the people, but they didn't understand what he meant.

**Yeshua** emphasized, "I can guarantee this truth: I am the gate for the sheep. All who came before I did were thieves or robbers. However, the sheep didn't respond to them. I am the gate. Those who enter the sheep pen through me will be saved. They will go in and out of the sheep pen and find food. A thief comes to steal, kill, and destroy. But I came so that my sheep will have life and so that they will have everything they need.

"I am the good shepherd. The good shepherd gives his life for the sheep. A hired hand isn't a shepherd and doesn't own the sheep. When he sees a wolf coming, he abandons the sheep and quickly runs away. So the wolf drags the sheep away and scatters the flock. The hired hand is concerned about what he's going to get paid and not about the sheep.

"I am the good shepherd. I know my sheep as the Father knows me. My sheep know me as I know the Father. So I give my life for my sheep. I also have other sheep that are not from this pen. I must lead them. They, too, will respond to my voice. So they will be one flock with one shepherd. The Father loves me because I give my life in order to take it back again. No one takes my life from me. I give my life of my own free will. I have the authority to give my life, and I have the authority to take my life back again. This is what my Father ordered me to do."

## UNDERSTANDING THE NAME

Scripture uses various metaphors to describe God's people—a temple, a body, a bride, a garden, a vineyard, or a flock of sheep. Shepherding, in fact, was an important occupation in ancient Israel. The role of the shepherd was to provide three things for the flock in his care: food, protection, and guidance.

Just as God's people are sometimes described in Scripture as a faithless bride, they are also pictured as a scattered flock. At such times, their leaders are portrayed as false shepherds who care little for the well-being of the flock entrusted to them. Without a shepherd to watch over them, the sheep scatter, becoming easy prey for wild animals and thieves.

Out of love for his wayward people, God promises to become their Shepherd. The book of Isaiah paints one of the most poignant images of God in the Hebrew Scriptures:

"He tends his flock like a shepherd:

He gathers the lambs in his arms and carries them close to his heart;

he gently leads those that have young." (Isaiah 40:11 NIV)

Jesus shows us the lengths to which he as the Good Shepherd, or *Poimen Kalos* (poi-MAIN ka-LOS), will go in order to protect his sheep. Unlike those who merely work for pay, Jesus will never abandon his sheep. Instead, he will defend them with his own life. After his resurrection, Jesus exhorted Peter to follow his example by feeding his sheep. Leaders of the early church were referred to as "pastor," another translation of the Greek word *poimen*.

# CONNECTING TO THE NAME

1. Why do you think Jesus describes his relationship to his people as that of Shepherd and sheep?

2. This passage from John 10 contains both frightening and comforting images. It is frightening to think that thieves, robbers, and wolves want to prey on the sheep, but comforting to know that Jesus will go to any lengths to protect them. How do these images express spiritual realities?

3. The phrase "good shepherd" implies that there are also bad shepherds. How is it possible to tell the difference?

4. Describe an experience in which you recognized the voice of the Good Shepherd in your own life.

5. Describe ways in which Jesus has watched over and protected you as your Shepherd, even when you have walked through the valley of the shadow of death.

6. Who in your life is like a lost sheep whom God is seeking? What can you do to help bring this person into his flock?

# PRAYING A PASSAGE WITH GOD'S NAME

Praise God for his constant care and protection and ask him for the grace to follow him closely. Pray, too, for your own pastors, who are trying to care for the flock Jesus has entrusted to them. Focus on the name *Poimen Kalos*, "Good Sheperd," as you read Psalm 23:1–4.

> 1 ***Yahweh*** is my ***Roeh***.
> I am never in need.
>> 2 He makes me lie down in green pastures.
>> He leads me beside peaceful waters.
>> 3 He renews my soul.
>> He guides me along the paths of righteousness
>>> for the sake of his name.
> 4 Even though I walk through the dark valley of death,
>> because you are with me, I fear no harm.
>> Your rod and your staff give me courage.

## PRAYING THE NAME **GOOD SHEPHERD** FOR MYSELF

Look up and read: Matthew 18:12–14

Read the parable of the shepherd who left his sheep to search after the lost one. Does his behavior strike you as strange? Have you ever imitated the Good Shepherd, searching after a lost loved one at the cost of other resources? Are there any lost sheep that God is calling you to go after now? Ask him to show you.

_____

_____

_____

_____

# PROMISES FROM THE **GOOD SHEPHERD**

In the past God spoke to our ancestors at many different times and in many different ways through the prophets. [2] In these last days he has spoken to us through his Son. God made his Son responsible for everything. His Son is the one through whom God made the universe. [3] His Son is the reflection of God's glory and the exact likeness of God's being. He holds everything together through his powerful words. After he had cleansed people from their sins, he received the highest position, the one next to the Father in heaven.

—Hebrews 1:1–3

> ***Adonay Yahweh*** is coming with power
>     to rule with authority.
>     His reward is with him,
>     and the people he has won arrive ahead of him.
> [11] Like a shepherd he takes care of his flock.
>     He gathers the lambs in his arms.
>     He carries them in his arms.
>     He gently helps the sheep and their lambs.
>     —Isaiah 40:10–11

## FOR DEEPER STUDY

*Read the following passages, considering the name* **GOOD SHEPHERD** *and how its meaning relates to the context of the passage.*

| | | |
|---|---|---|
| Psalm 23 | Isaiah 40:10–11 | Ezekiel 34:1–31 |
| Matthew 9:36; 25:31–33 | Luke 19:10 | John 21:15–19 |
| 1 Peter 2:24–25; 5:1–4 | | |

# SERVANT, SERVANT OF GOD, MAN OF SORROWS

אֶבֶד   *EBED*

παῖς τοῦ θεοῦ
*PAIS TOU THEOU*

אִישׁ מַכְאֹבוֹת
*ISH MAKOBOTH*

אִישׁ מַכְאֹבוֹת

Like most of us, Jesus' disciples were sometimes caught up with a sense of their own self-importance, at times even arguing with each other about which of them was greatest. Jesus startled them by reversing the natural order in which it is the weak who serve the strong. He assured them, instead, that he came not in order to control and dominate but in order to serve.

Though prophets, judges, and kings were called servants of God in the Bible, Jesus is the greatest of all God's servants, the Man of Sorrows who laid down his life in obedience to his Father. He is the Servant who through his suffering has saved us. When you pray to Jesus as Servant or as the Man of Sorrows, you are praying to the Lord who has loved you in the most passionate way possible, allowing himself to be nailed to a cross in order that you might have life and have it to the full.

## KEY SCRIPTURES

> He was despised and rejected by people.
>> He was an ***Ish Makoboth***, familiar with suffering.
>> He was despised like one from whom people turn their
>>> faces,
>>> and we didn't consider him to be worth anything.
> —Isaiah 53:3

It's the same way with the Son of Man. He didn't come so that others could serve him. He came to serve and to give his life as a ransom for many people.

—Matthew 20:28

# CHRIST REVEALS HIS NAME IN SCRIPTURE
## ISAIAH 52:13; 53:2–5; MATTHEW 20:26–28

*Open your personal Bible translation and read the same passage. Make note where you read* **SERVANT** *or* **SUFFERING**, *or where you see the name* **MAN OF SORROWS** *or* **MAN OF SUFFERING**.

My servant will be successful.
He will be respected, praised, and highly honored.

He grew up in his presence like a young tree,
like a root out of dry ground.
He had no form or majesty that would make us look at
him.
He had nothing in his appearance that would make us
desire him.
He was despised and rejected by people.
He was an *Ish Makoboth*, familiar with suffering.
He was despised like one from whom people turn their
faces,
and we didn't consider him to be worth anything.
He certainly has taken upon himself our suffering
and carried our sorrows,
but we thought that *Elohim* had wounded him,
beat him, and punished him.
He was wounded for our rebellious acts.
He was crushed for our sins.
He was punished so that we could have peace,
and we received healing from his wounds.

But that's not the way it's going to be among you. Whoever wants to become great among you will be your servant. Whoever wants to be most important among you will be your slave. It's the same way with the Son of Man. He didn't come so that others could serve him. He came to serve and to give his life as a ransom for many people."

אֶבֶד

# παῖς τοῦ θεοῦ

## UNDERSTANDING THE NAME

After God led the Israelites out of their slavery in Egypt, he did not treat them as slaves but as his own people, his sons and daughters. Though slavery was practiced in Israel, the Law forbade the forcible enslavement of freeborn individuals. To kidnap or sell such a person was to incur the death penalty. However, people could sell themselves in order to pay off their debts. Even so, Hebrew slaves were to be released after a certain number of years because no child of God was meant to live in perpetual bondage.

Though the Israelites were not considered God's slaves, they were considered his servants, freely putting his interests before their own, confident of his care and protection. To be God's servant involved living with an attitude of dependence and obedience. Scripture speaks of Moses, Joshua, Hannah, David, Isaiah, Mary the mother of Jesus, and many others as God's servants because they lived a life of faithful obedience.

The Servant Songs in Isaiah (42:1–4; 49:1–7; 50:4–9; 52:13–53:12) all speak of a mysterious Servant who would bring justice to the nations. Through his suffering this Man of Sorrows (ISH ma-ko-BOTH) would redeem many. The Jews may have understood this as a reference to Israel while early Christians understood these passages as messianic prophecies pointing to the suffering, death, and resurrection of Jesus Christ. By becoming one of us, Jesus suffered both with and for us. He was the Servant (E-bed) par excellence, the Servant of God (PICE tou the-OU), who not only obeyed God but obeyed to the point of death.

As his people, we are to follow his example, remembering his words that "whoever wants to become great among you must be your servant." Jesus' words make particular sense in light of the fact that in ancient times, a servant's status was directly related to the status of his master. To be a servant of the King of Kings, then, is the greatest of privileges. It is no surprise to discover that the word "minister," derived from a Latin word, and the word "deacon," derived from a Greek word, both mean "servant."

אִישׁ מַכְאֹבוֹת

# CONNECTING TO THE NAME

1. Describe an experience in which someone served you? How did it affect you?

2. Describe experiences in which you have been able to serve someone else with the love of Christ.

3. How does the passage from Isaiah fit or fail to fit with your image of Jesus?

4. The Man of Sorrows was unattractive, despised, and rejected. Imagine Jesus just prior to his death. See in his face sorrow and bitter grief for the world. What drove him to endure such suffering?

5. When you think of Jesus' suffering, how does it make you feel about him, about yourself, about others?

6. To be God's servant involves living with an attitude of humble dependence and obedience. How can this attitude be expressed in you?

# PRAYING A PASSAGE WITH GOD'S NAME

Thank God that we have been liberated from death because of the love of the one we call "Man of Sorrows." We have joy because of how he suffered on our behalf. Focus on the meaning of the names *Pais Tou Theou*, "Servant of God," and *Ish Makoboth*, "Man of Sorrows," as you read John 13:1–5.

> Before the Passover festival, **Yeshua** knew that the time had come for him to leave this world and go back to the Father. **Yeshua** loved his own who were in the world, and he loved them to the end.
>
> ² While supper was taking place, the devil had already put the idea of betraying **Yeshua** into the mind of Judas, son of Simon Iscariot.
>
> ³ The Father had put everything in **Yeshua's** control. **Yeshua** knew that. He also knew that he had come from God and was going back to God. ⁴ So he got up from the table, removed his outer clothes, took a towel, and tied it around his waist. ⁵ Then he poured water into a basin and began to wash the disciples' feet and dry them with the towel that he had tied around his waist.

## PRAYING THE NAMES SERVANT OF GOD AND MAN OF SORROW FOR MYSELF

Look up and read: Isaiah 53:2–5

Jesus, the Man of Sorrow, carried your sins to the cross. He was wounded for your iniquities. Are there any sins that you, in pride and shame, have not wanted him to carry for you? Confess this to him, and ask him for greater acceptance of sorrows in your own life.

_____

_____

_____

_____

# PROMISES FROM THE **SERVANT OF GOD** AND **MAN OF SORROWS**

Here is my *Ebed*, whom I support.
>Here is my chosen one, with whom I am pleased.
>I have put my *Ruach* on him.
>He will bring justice to the nations.
>²He will not cry out or raise his voice.
>He will not make his voice heard in the streets.
>³He will not break off a damaged cattail.
>He will not even put out a smoking wick.
>He will faithfully bring about justice.
>⁴He will not be discouraged or crushed
>until he has set up justice on the earth.
>The coastlands will wait for his teachings.
>—Isaiah 42:1-4

He will see and be satisfied
>because of his suffering.
>My righteous *Ebed* will acquit many people
>because of what he has learned through suffering.
>He will carry their sins as a burden.
>—Isaiah 53:11

## FOR DEEPER STUDY

*Read the following passages, considering the names* **SERVANT OF GOD,** *and* **MAN OF SORROWS** *and how its meaning relates to the context of the passage.*

Psalm 34:22

Matthew 12:15–21; 24:42–51

Philippians 2:3–11

Isaiah 49:5–6; 50:4–9; 52:13–53:12

1 Corinthians 9:19–23

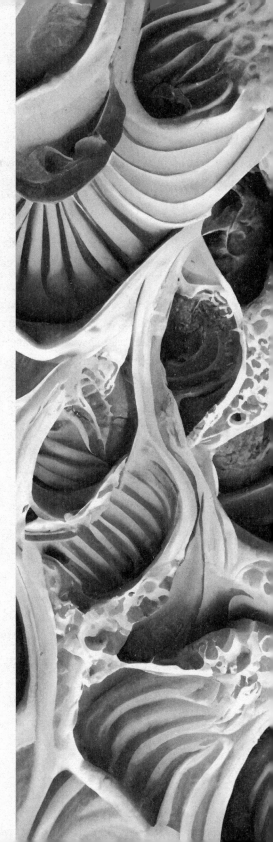

# THE REDEEMER

## גָּאַל GOEL
## λύτρον LYTRON

Without a Redeemer willing and able to pay the high price necessary to liberate us from the power of sin, the story of our lives in this world would be nothing but a story of hopelessness. But because of Christ's redemptive love, we look forward with hope to a day when the world itself will be completely liberated from the power of sin and death. Until then we can express our faith in Christ by echoing the words of Scripture: "I know that my redeemer lives and that in the end he will stand upon the earth. And . . . in my flesh I will see God" (Job 19:25–26 NIV).

## KEY SCRIPTURE

"It's the same way with the Son of Man. He didn't come so that others could serve him. He came to serve and to give his life as a ransom for many people."

—Mark 10:45

# CHRIST REVEALS HIS NAME IN SCRIPTURE
## PSALM 49:7–8; MARK 10:42, 45; REVELATION 5:9

*Open your personal Bible translation and read the same passages. Make note where you read the word* **REDEEMER***.*

No one can ever buy back another person

or pay **Elohim** a ransom for his life.

The price to be paid for his soul is too costly.

**Yeshua** called the apostles and said, "You know that the acknowledged rulers of nations have absolute power over people and their officials have absolute authority over people...

It's the same way with the Son of Man. He didn't come so that others could serve him. He came to serve and to give his life as a ransom for many people."

Then they sang a new song,

"You deserve to take the scroll and open the seals on it,

because you were slaughtered.

You bought people with your blood to be God's own.

They are from every tribe, language, people, and nation."

## UNDERSTANDING THE NAME

Redemption involves winning back, buying back, or repurchasing. The most dramatic example of this in the Old Testament was the exodus of God's people from Egypt. The former slaves praised *Yahweh* for acting as their Redeemer (Exodus 15:13). Subsequently, the prophets often linked redemption with freedom from political oppression.

But redemption also came into play within Israel itself because land, firstborn males, slaves, and people, objects, and animals consecrated to God all had to be redeemed by means of some kind of payment. In certain instances, such as when land had been sold to pay a debt (Leviticus 25:25–28) or a person had sold himself into slavery, the

λύτρον

person's closest relative, called the "kinsman redeemer," had the right to step in and pay off the debt so that the land could be returned or the person could be freed.

God is often called "Redeemer" (*Ga'al*; ga-AL) in the Old Testament. Though the New Testament never directly refers to Jesus as the Redeemer, it makes clear that he offered himself as a ransom or as redemption (*Lytron*; LU-tron) when he died on the cross. Rather than liberating his people from political oppression, as many expected the Messiah to do, Jesus came to free his people from the demonic powers to which sin had enslaved them. His blood was the purchase price, offered not to Satan but to the Father as the ultimate expression of his love. By giving his life for them and for us, Jesus didn't make light of our guilt but lifted us, as one commentator has said, "out of disobedience into his own obedience," thereby freeing us from the bondage of sin and remaking us in his image.

## CONNECTING TO THE NAME

1. Why is Jesus worthy of purchasing each of us for God?

2. If Christ the Redeemer has purchased you with his blood, what are the implications for your sense of selfworth? For your sense of the worth of others?

3. The passage from Revelation indicates that you were purchased *for* God. If that is so, what are the implications for your life?

4. Christ did not only free you from the slavery of sin, he also secured for you eternal life where you will be completely free from the ravages of sin, sickness, suffering, and sorrow. What do you look forward to seeing eradicated from your life? What do you envision attaining?

5. Scripture says that Jesus has purchased members from every tribe and language and people and nation. How diverse is your denomination or local church? Are you happy with the status quo? Why or why not?

## PRAYING A PASSAGE WITH GOD'S NAME

Praise Jesus because he is alive and active in our world. He is our great Redeemer who we will one day see face to face. Focus on the name *Go'el*, "Redeemer," as you read Job 19:25–26.

> But I know that my *Go'el* lives,
>     and afterwards, he will rise on the earth.
> [26] Even after my skin has been stripped off my body,
>     I will see *Eloah* in my own flesh.

### PRAYING THE NAME REDEEMER FOR MYSELF

Look up and read: Deuteronomy 7:8

Like the ancient Israelites, we, too, have been redeemed, freed from our slavery to sin. Write a prayer in praise to your Redeemer for bringing you out of your own personal Egypt and turning you to a land of promise, taking the verses below as inspiration.

_____

_____

_____

_____

# PROMISES FROM YOUR **REDEEMER**

⁴Don't be afraid, Jacob, you worm.
    You people of Israel, I will help you,"
    declares **Yahweh**, your **Go'el**, **Qedosh Yisrael**.
    —Isaiah 41:14

But **Elohim** will buy me back from the power of hell
    because he will take me.
    —Psalm 49:15

## FOR DEEPER STUDY

*Read the following passages, considering the name* **REDEEMER** *and how its meaning relates to the context of the passage.*

Psalm 130:7–8

Isaiah 54:5

Jeremiah 50:33–34

Luke 1:67–75; 21:25–28

Ephesians 1:3–10

Revelation 5:6–9

# I AM

## אֶהְיֶה or ἐγώ εἰμι
### EHYEH or EGO EIMI

In Jesus we have the richest, most vivid picture of God imaginable. No longer does God seem implacably remote, displeased with the world he has made. Instead, he bends toward us, sharing our weakness and shouldering our burdens. Through the perfect offering of his life he becomes our Way back to the Father. He is the true Vine in which we abide, bearing fruit for God's kingdom. He is the loving God who will never abandon us, but who will be present with us always, leading us to life eternal.

## KEY SCRIPTURES

Then Moses replied to **Elohim**, "Suppose I go to the people of Israel and say to them, 'The **Elohim** of your ancestors has sent me to you,' and they ask me, 'What is his name?' What should I tell them?"

**Elohim** answered Moses, "**Ehyeh** Who **Ehyeh**. This is what you must say to the people of Israel: '**Ehyeh** has sent me to you.'"

—Exodus 3:13–14

The Jews said to **Jesus**, "You're not even fifty years old. How could you have seen Abraham?" **Jesus** told them, "I can guarantee this truth: Before Abraham was ever born, I am."

—John 8:57–58

# CHRIST REVEALS HIS NAME IN SCRIPTURE
## EXODUS 3:13–14, JOHN 8:50–59

*Open your personal Bible translation and read the same passages. Make note where you read* **EHYEH** *or* **I AM**.

Then Moses replied to **Elohim**, "Suppose I go to the people of Israel and say to them, 'The **Elohim** of your ancestors has sent me to you,' and they ask me, 'What is his name?' What should I tell them?"

**Elohim** answered Moses, "**Ehyeh** Who **Ehyeh**. This is what you must say to the people of Israel: '**Ehyeh** has sent me to you.'"

I don't want my own glory. But there is someone who wants it, and he is the judge. I can guarantee this truth: Whoever obeys what I say will never see death."

The Jews told **Yeshua**, "Now we know that you're possessed by a demon. Abraham died, and so did the prophets, but you say, 'Whoever does what I say will never taste death.' Are you greater than our father Abraham, who died? The prophets have also died. Who do

you think you are?"

**Yeshua** said, "If I bring glory to myself, my glory is nothing. My Father is the one who gives me glory, and you say that he is your God. Yet, you haven't known him. However, I know him. If I would say that I didn't know him, I would be a liar like all of you. But I do know him, and I do what he says. Your father Abraham was pleased to see that my day was coming. He saw it and was happy."

The Jews said to **Yeshua**, "You're not even fifty years old. How could you have seen Abraham?"

**Yeshua** told them, "I can guarantee this truth: Before Abraham was ever born, I am."

Then some of the Jews picked up stones to throw at **Yeshua**. However, **Yeshua** was concealed, and he left the temple courtyard.

## UNDERSTANDING THE NAME

When Moses first encountered God in the wilderness in the figure of a burning bush, he asked God to reveal his name. But the reply he received seemed only to add to the mystery of who God is. Instead of describing himself as the Living God or the Almighty God or the Everlasting God or the Creator God, the Lord instructed Moses, saying, "This is what you are to say to the Israelites: 'I am has sent me to you.' " In fact, the name "I am" is closely related to the four Hebrew consonants that make up the name *Yahweh*, the covenant name of God in the Old Testament. Though the exact meaning of this name is difficult to know with certainty, the Lord may have been revealing himself not only as the God who has always existed but also as the God who is always present with his people.

When Jesus was being attacked by the religious leaders who failed to recognize him as the Messiah, he shocked them not by claiming to be the Messiah but by identifying himself with *Yahweh*, saying: "Before Abraham was born, *I am*." Recognizing that Jesus was claiming to be divine, the scandalized religious leaders tried to stone him. In fact, John's gospel contains several self-descriptions of Jesus introduced by the emphatic expression *Ego Eimi* (e-GO ay-MEE), "I am."

I am the bread of life. (6:35)

I am the light of the world. (8:12)

Before Abraham was born, I am. (8:58)

I am the gate for the sheep. (10:7)

I am the good shepherd. (10:11)

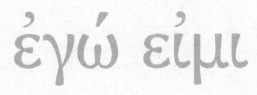

I am the resurrection and the life. (11:25)

I am the way and the truth and the life. (14:6)

I am the true vine, and my Father is the gardener. (15:1)

Jesus emphatically described himself as the "resurrection and the life," "the way and the truth and the life," and the "true vine." Each of these images has something important to reveal to us about the character and purpose of Jesus Christ.

# CONNECTING TO THE NAME

1. Some scholars think that by saying "I am who I am," God was saying he would always be present with his people. How have you experienced God's faithful presence in your life?

2. Why do you think the religious leaders responded to the "good news" as though it were "bad news"?

3. What do Jesus' words teach us about his presence through time?

4. Before his crucifixion, Jesus revealed himself to his disciples, saying, "I am the way and the truth and the life." What is Jesus the way to?

5. In John 15:1–5 Jesus speaks of himself as the true vine and calls us to remain in him. What does it mean to "remain in the vine"? Think about your hardships in the light of "pruning."

# PRAYING A PASSAGE WITH GOD'S NAME

The power of Christ in this most vulnerable moment is astonishing. Feel the awe as you imagine Jesus, with all the power of God, allowing his enemies to take him captive. Focus on the name *Ego Eimi*, "I Am," as you read John 18:4–6.

> [4] **Yeshua** knew everything that was going to happen to him. So he went to meet them and asked, "Who are you looking for?"
>
> [5] They answered him, "**Yeshua** from Nazareth."
>
> **Yeshua** told them, "I am he."
>
> Judas, who betrayed him, was standing with the crowd. [6] When **Yeshua** told them, "I am he," the crowd backed away and fell to the ground.

## PRAYING THE NAME **I AM** FOR MYSELF

Look up and read: John 14:1–6

Jesus, the great I Am, is preparing a place for you, a place as real as he is. What do you hope that he—the way, the truth, and the life—has in store for you? It will be better than any of us can imagine.

_____

_____

_____

_____

## PROMISES FROM THE GREAT **I AM**

[21]Martha told **Yeshua**, "Lord, if you had been here, my brother would not have died. [22]But even now I know that God will give you whatever you ask him."

[23] **Yeshua** told Martha, "Your brother will come back to life."

[24]Martha answered **Yeshua**, "I know that he'll come back to life on the last day, when everyone will come back to life."

[25] **Yeshua** said to her, "I am the one who brings people back to life, and I am life itself. Those who believe in me will live even if they die. [26]Everyone who lives and believes in me will never die. Do you believe that?"

—John 11:21-26

### FOR DEEPER STUDY

*Read the following passages, considering the name **I AM** and how its meaning relates to the context of the passage.*

Matthew 16:15–16; 28:20

Mark 14:61–62

Revelation 1:8

# Praying the Names of Jesus

*Ann Spangler*

# Praying the Names of God

*Ann Spangler*

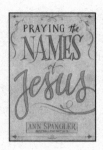

Names in the ancient world did more than simply distinguish one person from another; they often conveyed the essential nature and character of a person. This is especially true when it comes to the names of God recorded in the Bible. *Praying the Names of God* explores the primary names and titles of God in the Old Testament to reveal the deeper meanings behind them. *Praying the Names of Jesus* does the same thing for Jesus in the New Testament.

By understanding the biblical context in which these names and titles are revealed, readers gain a more intimate knowledge of Jesus and of his plan for their lives.

*Available in stores and online!*